SHAPE & CARE YOUR PUPPY'S LIFE

TRAINING AND NUTRITION FOR A PERFECT DOG

ALEX GREY

CONTENTS

Introduction — vii

1. WELCOMING A NEW PUPPY HOME — 1
- Preparation — 2
- Purchase the Essentials — 7
- Picking Up Your New Puppy — 17
- Collecting Your Puppy — 18
- Traveling in the Car — 22
- Introducing Your Puppy to Their New Home — 23
- Establishing a Routine — 27

2. ESSENTIAL TRAINING — 31
- Potty Training — 32
- Routine — 36
- Sleeping Arrangements — 42
- The First Night — 46
- Going Out for Walks — 50
- Walking Issues to Address — 53

3. BASIC COMMANDS — 58
- Commands — 67
- Post Training Essentials — 76

4. NUTRITION AND HEALTH — 78
- Dog Health Essentials — 79
- Grooming Essentials — 82
- Spaying and Neutering: — 87
- Signs of Health Problems in a Puppy — 89
- The Signs — 90
- Common Puppy Diseases — 94
- Nutrition Essentials — 97

5. STORE-BOUGHT OR HOMEMADE FOOD	104
Homemade Puppy Food	106
Types of Homemade Dog Diets	113
Homemade Puppy Food and Treat Recipes:	115
Store-Bought Foods	121
Meeting Your Pup's Nutritional Needs	125
6. BEHAVIORAL PROBLEMS AND DOG COMMUNICATION	127
Common Behavioral Issues	128
Other Common Behaviors	143
Canine Body Language	145
Afterword	151
References	155

© Copyright 2020 - All rights reserved.

The content contained within this book may not be reproduced, duplicated or transmitted without direct written permission from the author or the publisher.

Under no circumstances will any blame or legal responsibility be held against the publisher, or author, for any damages, reparation, or monetary loss due to the information contained within this book, either directly or indirectly.

Legal Notice:

This book is copyright protected. It is only for personal use. You cannot amend, distribute, sell, use, quote or paraphrase any part, or the content within this book, without the consent of the author or publisher.

Disclaimer Notice:

Please note the information contained within this document is for educational and entertainment purposes only. All effort has been executed to present accurate, up to date, reliable, complete information. No warranties of any kind are declared or implied. Readers acknowledge that the author is not engaged in the rendering of legal, financial, medical or professional advice. The content within this book has been derived from various sources. Please consult a licensed professional before attempting any techniques outlined in this book.

By reading this document, the reader agrees that under no circumstances is the author responsible for any losses, direct or indirect, that are incurred as a result of the use of the information contained within this document, including, but not limited to, errors, omissions, or inaccuracies.

❀ Created with Vellum

INTRODUCTION

"Dogs do speak, but only to those who know how to listen."

-by Orhan Pamuk

Bringing a puppy home is a significant milestone; a wonderful experience you will undergo either as an individual or as a family. That being said, many dog owners are unclear about the individual care routine their new companion will need. Should you be domineering? How many commands does your puppy need to know? Are puppies allowed on the couch? Or in the bed? Are crates necessary or cruel? How can you be a master and a friend at the same time? What nutrition does puppy food contain? How much does a chihuahua eat? How many walks does your puppy need?

Introduction

You are smart to ask these questions, and I suspect you have many more.

Puppy care is a much debated and discussed topic. Throughout this book I want to broaden your perception about puppies, how they develop and how you can assist them. We will look at the physical transformation puppies go through, and how this will influence your care choices. I will also delve into psychological qualities, and how you can use these to further understand your puppy.

Many times dog owners will be left wondering why their efforts and attempts will fall short of expectations. It takes much more than just crossing your fingers and hoping for the best. Different breeds often require different care patterns, for example. Like caring for a child, age and personality are factors that will affect your choices. You'll learn how to comprehend these components to make accurate training decisions.

There are always pitfalls when we get the notion into our heads that we are ready for a puppy. These puppy pitfalls can be avoided if you understand the difference between your puppy's capabilities and your own expectations. If you rely entirely on theory, without trying to read the signals of the puppy in front of you, then your efforts will be in vain. I encourage you to have patience and build up a personalized approach that fits your puppy's breed and personality.

It's key that you do not neglect this responsibility. Carelessness can creep up on a dog owner easily. It goes without saying that you should weigh up the commitment you are about to undertake. With a puppy (or any other pet) understand that you are investing in a lifelong obligation to love and attending to their needs. We are as responsible for their suffering as we are for their happiness. Without engaging mental stimulation, consistent training and correct nutrition, a puppy can become distressed and unhappy.

Shape & Care Your Puppy's Life is not a quick fix, or a "train your dog to be brilliant in twenty-four hours" class. It's something you will both work towards for the rest of your dog's life. The goal is to help your dog live peacefully; to teach them to respect their environment and the people they live alongside. A good dog and good training is more than a few well executed commands, or unyielding obedience. You must really consider what you wish to do with your puppy, and how training will enable them to behave accordingly. How will you set up effective communication and reinforce your dog meaningfully?

Introduction

I grew up in a household that truly appreciated the bond between human and dog. There was not one time in my childhood that I did not have a fluffy, enthusiastic wet-nosed companion. I felt luckier than most children I knew in my neighborhood, because a significant number of my friends were forbidden from having dogs; either from their own or their parents' aversion to dogs, allergies or no space at home. Dogs and animals were prevalent in my childhood.

Every new addition to our family, even the ones that followed an incomprehensible and painful loss, reaffirmed the connection that me and my family felt toward the domestic dog. They were family; a shared responsibility. Every puppy brought with it a world of possibilities, delightful memories, significant bonding experiences and learning curves. Not every dog was quite like the last, which made each relationship, and the way my family and I approached training, that little bit more unique.

There were times I faced great hardships in life. Having suffered in both my professional and personal life, I cannot truly relay to you the value of having my dog during these times. To say that the bond of love between us was unconditional is an understatement. It was elevating - pushing me to be strong and to pull through my misery. This is not to say a puppy, a dog, or a pet should be viewed as a source of therapy. This is

Introduction

an expectation that asks too much from our companions, and can be detrimental to forming a healthy relationship with them. We still have an obligation to be their leaders, which is where I chose to focus my energy - that was my drive. To be the best owner I could be.

A dog can add profound joy to your life. It's a connection no one should ever take for granted. It's why I've dedicated my working life to exploring the particulars of dog training. I sought help to navigate this fascinating and rewarding topic, and underwent extensive reeducation. The process was enlightening, and encouraged further analysis of the psychology of puppies. What causes a pet to act a certain way? How can we influence good behavior? What I want to share with you is the outcome of my research. By the end of this book, I hope that you will feel well-equipped and worthy of the puppy you are about to introduce into the topsy-turvy human world.

Life with a new puppy will be challenging, there's no question about it. They will need all the support and help you can offer to become a content and healthy pet. Grasping how they process the world, how our actions and guidance can influence them will be the focus of this guide book. With an over flux of how-to guide books, and information available to us on raising a puppy, it is easy for a new owner to second guess their decisions. The advice out there can be conflicting and contradictory. Everyone has their own nugget of advice to offer you. The breeder or rescue center tells you one thing, the vet tells you another, your neighbor says something different entirely. Choosing the best approach can become dizzying.

As you go through *The Puppy Guide* you'll quickly learn that puppy training is a journey of trial and error. I have many complex leads, harnesses, training clickers, whistles and agility equipment to attest to this. Throughout this guide book you will find a breed and age specific models to help alleviate your uncertainty. We want the best for our dogs, we want to know the best practices and the most effective training techniques. Whether you are a first time owner, or a seasoned one, in this guide book you will discover:

- Straightforward easy to follow approaches for teaching a dog basic commands.
- Disciplinary advice and positive reinforcement practices for your puppy.
- How to calm restless, barky and stubborn dogs.
- Leash training.
- Potty training.
- How to interact with your puppy positively.

- Troubleshooting health concerns and how to appropriately address them.
- Proper nutrition for various ages and breeds.
- The best grooming practices dependent on breed.
- Introducing the dog in social settings, with friends, family, children and other dogs.
- How to form a systematic approach to tackle training inconsistency.
- How to avoid overindulging your new puppy.
- How to form structure, secure leadership and reliability on a daily basis.

While it may seem like a lot to consider at first, and you wouldn't be wrong to feel nervous, remember that in time and with practice these choices and methods will become second nature to you. Implementing the best training techniques early on will ensure that you will raise a wonderful, well-adjusted puppy, as studies on the matter have shown that a "positive response to strangers in the Puppy Class group was significantly higher than that in the Adult Class and No Class groups...Puppy Class may help prevent canine behavioral problems such as disobedience or fear of strangers." (Kutsumi et al, 2012, p.1)

Early training will help you to troubleshoot behavioral issues prior to them becoming burdensome and

Introduction

dangerous. You will teach them boundaries and rules and gain confidence in showing them the world without fear of misbehavior. A puppy with good behavior will get to experience more of the world, gain greater stimulation and interaction from others. Help your puppy have these engaging opportunities. Training ties into every aspect of their development. So it is key that you prioritize your puppy training in their early life.

Start their training off on the right path to strengthen your friendship with your new puppy, and it will grow into a happy life-long relationship. Show your puppy that the safest place for them is in your hands.

CHAPTER 1

WELCOMING A NEW PUPPY HOME

There's no disputing that bringing a new puppy home is an exciting and wonderful time. You may be thinking purely about the games you'll play, the places you'll take them, all the cuddles and belly rubs you have to offer. However, the transition from one environment to another can be stressful on a new puppy.

Moving to a new home, the puppy may be distraught from being removed from its familiar environment. That is why it is essential for the first few days to run as smoothly as possible, so that your puppy may settle in. A fun and exciting prospect can turn badly very quickly if you, as a new owner, are not prepared. This move requires more forethought than you might imagine. Leaving anything unchecked or to the last minute will also be a significant source of stress on you. As the saying goes, fail to prepare, prepare to fail.

When families discover that they will be welcoming a child into the household, there are months of detailed preparation predating the arrival. However, the prospect of bringing a puppy home is usually executed on a whim, with little thought as to what they should do and why. It's little wonder that this can lead to setbacks in bonding, and training. What you do, or fail to do in these first few days can determine the routine you and your puppy will fall into.

This first chapter will provide you with the best strategies for integrating your puppy into their new home. You will learn how to comfort your new puppy, socialize them, introduce structure to family members, detailing their specific responsibilities in puppy care, and of course picking out the essentials. By following this advice, the first days with your new puppy will be as uncomplicated as possible.

Preparation

Now that you know your new puppy will be arriving soon, a few days of preparation will be crucial.

Arrange time off work

Before you even step foot near the shelter to collect your puppy, it is good for you to get into the habit of making sacrifices, compromises and time commitments. Your willingness to do this is going to play a big role in your approach to puppy care. Consider this... if you were bringing a baby home, would you go to work the very next day? Puppies are required to stay with their mothers for the first eight weeks of their life. Until then, they are surrounded by their siblings, their parents and any other caretakers providing them with much-needed attention. Remember, your home is a stranger's home to your puppy; leaving them to process this foreign landscape alone can be distressing for them. Now that you are taking them from that comfort it is your responsibility to be their full-time companion and be at the forefront of introducing them to their new home.

If you are to be their sole care-taker, ideally you should take time off work to get them settled. This will not be time to do any extensive training; searching new surroundings and meeting new people will quickly wear a puppy out. Utilize this time for introducing them to the family, playing in and exploring their new playground. It is crucial that the primary caretaker welcome the puppy, and take on this role.

Have a family meeting

As I have said before, a puppy is a massive commitment. If you are part of a family, this new addition will impact all of your lives. It's important for you to have unity when it comes to caring for the new puppy. Be sure that everyone wants to be a part of this new adventure and that they are all willing to help.

Introducing a puppy to a family unit comes with various benefits; already there is a substantial group of people for the puppy to socialize and play with. There are also more hands-on-deck when it comes to daily care.

First, start by deciding who will be the puppy's primary caretaker. Yes, there will be assistance from the family, but the puppy is that person's puppy - therefore the brunt of the responsibility comes down to them. I assume that since you're reading this book, that person will be you! As the primary caretaker, you should be in charge of:

- Training (something that you implement and then share with the family)
- Veterinary responsibilities (scheduling appointments, vaccinations, etc.)
- Exercise (even if you are not doing the walking, make sure it is being done)
- Feeding (setting up a schedule and making sure it is adhered to)

As a family you can share responsibilities, of course. In fact, it's critical when it comes to the above that you are all on the same page.

Walking

The size and breed of your puppy will play a factor in how much exercise is required. In the first few weeks, exercise may be limited to playing in the house and in the yard while your puppy waits for their vaccinations. This is an activity you can all participate in as a group or individually. Perhaps there is a particular member in your family who is very active. Try to get everyone involved as your puppy will find it comforting to have familiar faces about them in the big outdoors. We will discuss, in-depth, a walking routine, later in this chapter.

Feeding

As the primary caretaker, it is your responsibility to know what nutrition your puppy needs (a topic we will discuss in Chapter Five). However, once you have put together a meal plan, you can share the specifics with the family. Feeding time will also become an opportunity to teach your puppy some meal manners; brief each family member on the process of having the puppy sitting down, laying down, shaking paw and/or making eye contact before their meal.

House rules

Lastly, this will be an opportune time to establish a set of puppy rules. With so many family members to listen to, a puppy will become easily confused if you are not all on the same page. Remember dogs have instincts and natural tendencies, some of which will not be appropriate in the household. As humans, we have a tendency to let the adorable new addition get away with pretty much anything. "Just this one time!" can easily turn into many times. As a family discuss, from day-one, what is absolutely not acceptable:

- Are there rooms off-limits?
- Where will the puppy be allowed in the house?
- Where will the puppy's sleeping place be?
- Who is responsible for what?
- What are the morning and evening routines?
- Will the puppy be allowed on the bed or the couch?

If you have a family with small children, it is also useful to set up rules for them on safety and acceptable behavior around the puppy. For instance:

- Let the puppy eat peacefully.

- Teach them how to handle a puppy; it is not a toy.
- Do not physically harm or scream at the dog.

Remember inconsistency is the biggest error in dog training, so make sure everyone is clear on the rules. Include the family in the decisions; if everyone agrees on the rules it will be easier for them to follow.

Purchase the Essentials

Before the puppy arrives in your home, make sure that you have the essential supplies to get you through the first few days. Buying the basics ahead of time will help your puppy settle immediately, without any panicked trips to the store. It will also help you relax, knowing that everything is already under your roof. The following is a checklist to help you get started.

Crate: The size of your crate is again dependent on the size of the puppy. You will have to factor in your dog's individual weight and size characteristics. The crate should be spacious enough for your puppy to sit, lay down and turn comfortably. There are crates that come with additional inserts, allowing you to adjust the size as the puppy grows. Having a crate that is too big allows your puppy extra space, which they might use as a toilet.

Having one that is too small will deter them from using that space as their own. Their crate should be used as a tool for calming their anxiety and having personal space. There are various materials used for crates; some will be more appropriate for specific breeds and uses:

- Wire
- Plastic
- Soft sided
- Wooden

Bedding: To encourage your pet to enjoy their new space, it is vital that the bedding is primarily soft and clean. For your own sanity, make sure that the material used for their bedding is durable and easy to wash. Potty accidents will be common in the first few weeks.

Covers and throws for your car: As you travel with your pup, a crate will be useful for designating space for them. A car seat belt can also ensure that they are safe and secure. Using throws will help to keep your car dirt and damage free. It will also retain your puppy's scent; they will know that their area is wherever the throw is.

Leash and collar: Puppies grow quickly; very soon that first collar will be too small for them, but it is essential for their safety and training that they have it. Choose a collar that is appropriate for the width of your puppy's neck, and material that is durable for their breed. A test you can do to ensure the fit is good is placing two fingers between your puppy's neck and their collar. Most collars will be adjustable, so you can lengthen them to an appropriate size. If in doubt, speak to a veterinarian or pet shop owner about the best fit and make for your puppy's breed.

Grooming supplies: Grooming is an essential part of puppy care. This extends from brushing, bathing to visiting the dog groomers to have you puppy clipped. Brushing is important for removing dead hair and grime from your puppy; they are going to be adventurous and curious outdoors so expect a lot of dirt. It will help keep their skin healthy and happy. Grooming will be a great way of keeping track of your dog's general health (be sure to look at their eyes, nails and teeth). This will help to identify any issues, such as lumps, scrapes, and soreness quickly. Brushing should be started immediately and implemented into your puppy's daily routine. This gets them used to the process, and accustomed to being handled, which reduces their stress during veterinary examinations.

As with all puppy accessories and essentials, there are many brushes and grooming kits on the market. Puppy fur is softer and fluffier than adult dogs; therefore, use a soft brush. A few grooming options you can look into are:

- Bristle Brushes - A versatile brush that can be used on any type of fur. Primarily used to brush the top coat The bristles will be dispersed differently for different types of hair.
- Close-together bristles: short-haired dogs
- Wider apart bristles: better for long-haired dogs
- Grooming Mitt - Better for short-haired dogs, and useful for removing dirt and dead hair.
- Undercoat Rake - A lot of first time dog owners only focus on grooming the topcoat of a puppy. In reality, a lot of mats and tangles form on the undercoat. Removing this actually benefits the top coat. Make sure the bristles and pins match your puppy's hair length. Longer bristles will penetrate a thick and lengthy coat, shorter ones are suitable for shorter hair.
- Rubber Brushes - They are less irritable on your puppy's skin and are good for massaging them.
- Slicker Brush - Perfect for getting rid of loose hair, maintaining a healthy condition for your puppy's coat. Angled pins can avoid harming the skin while still reaching the entirety of the puppy's coat. Always be gentle using this brush; the thin tightly spaced wires can be

uncomfortable if you apply too much pressure.

Just like us, it is good for your puppy to have regular oral hygiene. Starting this care routine early will benefit your puppy throughout their life. Your puppy will develop a full set of temporary teeth at four weeks old, these will eventually fall out and a new adult set will form by around 4-5 months; almost double the number of baby teeth.

Dental problems can form early in your puppy's life. Keep an eye out for bad breath, eating difficulties, swollen gums, blood in saliva, broken teeth, and infections (as these can spread to other parts of your puppy's body).

You can maintain your puppy's oral health by:

- Brushing their teeth with a specifically formulated puppy toothpaste. It's good for them to be comfortable with people pressing fingers into their mouths. This encourages calm behavior for future examinations.
- Chew toys are not just for entertainment. The right kind of chew toy will assist teething, quell their chewing urges and remove tartar build up.
- Dietary products can also have a cleansing

benefit (a topic we will discuss in detail in Chapter 4).

ID tags: One piece of essential equipment throughout your dog's life is an identification tag. It is not uncommon for them to slip their leash, run away out of fear or panic, or are even stolen in some cases. Should any of these happen (and I pray for you that they won't) an ID tag will be your puppy's best chance of finding their way safely home.

Dog tags will have room for a few lines of text on the front and back. Vital information you should include is:

- Your name
- A phone number where you can easily be reached
- Your street name and home address
- A note saying that you dog has a microchip

Adding your puppy's name is optional, but not essential. Dog theft is not uncommon; if a thief knows your dog's name then it is easier for them to pass the dog off as their own, or to pass it on to an unsuspecting owner, as your puppy will respond to their name.

Toys: Puppies need plenty of toys! These are not just for fun or a luxury item. They are a necessity. Toys will play a key role in assisting your puppy's training, mental stimulation and development. Toys are a great tool for socializing with your dog, for exercising them and reducing their stress and boredom. A toy is a great comfort to anxiety and will stifle behavioral problems early on.

Make sure that the toys you select are the appropriate size for your puppy. Toys that are too big will be off-putting, or even dangerous. A small-shaped toy can easily become lodged in a puppy's throat. The size of the puppy will also impact the material you select.

- Large and heavy jaws - need tougher materials to withstand rougher play.
- Small gentle jaws - will appreciate a softer fabric; something that is easier to grasp, for example a stuffed toy.

Consider the breed of your dog, as different toys will appeal to your puppy's individual characteristics. Puppies that do not have toys that engage their characteristics will become bored. Their toys should motivate them.

Retriever dogs - Retriever dogs are bred as "gun dogs" or working dogs. They are bred to retrieve game or animals that their owners hunted in the wild. Dogs such as golden retrievers, spaniels, and collies will appreciate a toy that they can fetch, as they have an innate instinct for bringing items back. Consider a ball or a Frisbee.

Scent hounds - Again another dog bred for hunting, these dogs have a reliance on their sense of smell. Born with larger nasal cavities, they process more information using their nose. A scent-based toy, such as a toy with a treat concealed inside, will help develop their sense of smell and boost their capacity to problem-solve.

Herder dogs - Bred to round up sheep and other animals, this is a dog that will appreciate an interactive toy. Consider purchasing an electronic toy (a smart ball or sensor toy) to keep their minds active.

Terrier dogs - These dog breeds tend to be on the small side, but have bundles of energy to burn. Initially bred as a hunting breed, they have a wealth of stamina. They have an innate intelligence, and were bred to stalk and track down other animals. Puzzle toys, such as treat dispensers, will give them a daily challenge to solve.

Keep in mind the activity level of your puppy's breed. While all dogs enjoy chewing their toys, for some it is important to increase their physical activity. In this case, purchase toys that require them to run wild outdoors.

Keeping the toys you purchase for your puppy will be no easy task; they will destroy and damage a lot of them as they grow. Adding a toy rotation into their routine will ensure that the toys you purchase will last longer.

The list I recommend for all first-time owners would be:

- Tennis balls
- Frisbee
- Treat dispensing toys
- A fabric toy (something that they can chew and snuggle up next to)
- A tug toy
- Interactive toys

Home proofing: Your home is about to become a playground. Your new puppy will have boundless amounts of curiosity, which is both a good and a bad thing. There may be dangers in your home that you are not entirely aware of, and will need to shield you puppy from

Gates: Keep the puppy in a designated area and away from places in the house you may not want them to go.

Child locks: Your puppy is very much like a child. To prevent them from sneaking into floor-level cupboards (containing food, cleaning products or clothing), fit a child lock to keep them securely closed

Chewables and damageables: Your little puppy will be tearing through the house; they don't always begin with a great concept of their speed and size. Try to remove things that they might easily run into, knock over or break. Any cushions, shoes, electrical cables and rugs may be a temptation for their teeth, so keep these out of the way as much as possible to begin with.

Plants: Some species of household plants are toxic, to both humans and animals. Their natural pollen and residue is particularly harmful to curious chew-happy puppies. If you have any houseplants on the floor, or within the puppy's reach, either remove them from the house entirely or up onto a higher level. Your puppy won't always have a desire to chew, but until they know better, this is the safest action.

Toys: Will keep puppies teeth away from chair legs, sofas and doors.

Toilet lid: Find ways to keep the toilet lid locked down; a puppy won't be able to resist and it's a bad habit you should prevent early as possible.

Food and water bowls: The bowl you'll need comes down to a matter of size and material. A large food bowl will be daunting to a little dog, and may make you prone to overfilling it. Buy a bowl size that is correct for them. If you do decide to buy a larger one (preparing for their growth), also purchase a dispenser to measure the correct amount of food for their weight. The size of the water bowl doesn't matter as much - the most important aspect is that your puppy has access to clean, fresh water at all times.

Food and a food container: Every puppy will need the correct source of nutrition for their growing pattern. A lot of growth will take place in the first few months, and quality food will help replenish lost energy and support proper development. This is a topic we will explore in greater detail in Chapter Five.

The food you purchase may come in large quantities; it is important for taste and nutritional benefit to keep their food fresh. A metallic or plastic food bin that seals tightly is a great place to store puppy's food. This type of bin blocks out oxygen and sunlight, which can cause the food to spoil; it also keeps out a curious, hungry puppy.

Picking Up Your New Puppy

Now that you have scoured the stores, prepared the house and the family, it is time to collect your puppy and bring them to their new home. This moving process will be exhilarating and unnerving for your new pup. This next section offers advice for making the journey there and back as painless and stress-free as possible.

Preparing the car

First and foremost, make sure the ride in the car will be comfortable for your puppy. I remember back to my teenage years, when my parents and I collected our family puppy. It was a two-hour-long journey from the shelter in the middle of winter. So, naturally we had the car heaters on full-blast. Due to a lack of ventilation, our puppy became dehydrated from the heat in the car, and the overall excitement caused him to be sick. When possible, turn the heaters off as you travel or keep the windows open for fresh air. Keep a crate in the car for when your puppy is traveling, or have someone there to hold them as you drive.

Collecting Your Puppy

Before arriving at the shelter, or breeder you are collecting your puppy from, take time to prepare some questions that will help with initial care. A breeder for a specific type of puppy will have all of the knowledge of rearing them, so it is good to seek advice about your specific puppy breed. Whoever has been caring for your puppy in the first few weeks will have observed them closely. There's a wealth of information they can offer you. All the excitement of picking the puppy up may overwhelm you, so consider the following questions before you leave:

Feeding schedule: Your puppy may have already been introduced to a feeding timetable. Knowing how much food, at what time and how many times a day they are to be fed will help with forming a routine. Puppies may not always be started on the food that is best for their nutritional needs. It is likely that you will want to change them over to different food. You will have to wean them off what they know, and transition them slowly onto something new; an immediate change can upset their tummies. A breeder for a specific breed may have recommendations, as well. Sometimes they will provide a dietary sheet to take home. I will also cover nutrition later in the book, to help you decide.

Previous veterinary care: Whether coming from a breeder or a shelter, it is important to know your puppy's medical history. It gives a clear indication of where you will need to start from in terms of vet care and health checks. Have they had any vaccinations? Worming treatments? Or developing health issues? Some puppies from shelters will have specific needs for health ailments. You may also be electing to care for a special-needs dog, in which case knowing their medical routine is essential.

Comforts: Puppies are prone to howling and crying, and will be even more so when you take them to an unfamiliar place. They may suffer separation anxiety, and their howling is a means of communicating that to you. Ask the breeder or shelter what comforts you can offer to help settle the puppy into his or her new home. It could be a case of tiring them out before bedtime, keeping their sleeping crate somewhere close to people, so they don't feel alone. Cozy blankets and bedding can also have a soothing effect.

Sleeping arrangements: Your breeder or shelter have closely observed your puppy in its first few weeks, and it's likely they will have already gotten them into a daily rhythm. Ask your breeder about sleeping times. Does your puppy already have a bedtime? What sort of plan or actions should you take to help your puppy sleep? Again the amount they sleep is dependent on their breed. Your puppy will sleep a lot in its first few weeks. This sleep time should always be undisturbed.

Breed specifics: When you are face-to-face with your puppy's breeder, it is a good time to quiz them about rearing the breed of puppy you have chosen. What dietary and grooming requirements should you take into consideration? What training will they require? Is your puppy prone to any specific behaviors? They are more than happy to offer advice to a new owner. Breeders want their dogs to be superior animals, and ensure that they are in top shape: "Responsible breeders have their breeding animals genetically tested for hereditary defects common to their specific breed, and will provide proof of such testing to parties interested in purchasing puppies from them." (Kramer, 2019, para 2)

Your puppy's history: If you have chosen to adopt from a shelter, a wonderful and fulfilling decision, it is important for you to take in as much information about your puppy's past. This will inform your future interactions with them, and how you can best adhere to their behavioral needs.

What social experiences has your puppy had?: In most cases, your puppy will have been confined to interactions with their parents, their siblings, other potential buyers and the breeder. An older puppy will have had more exposure to other people and animals. The breeder may have already begun teaching basic commands, but your approach to training may vary from theirs. This is okay. A shelter puppy may have not had a lot of social interaction with people and other dogs. It is a good idea to take note of their behavior and temperament in these situations.

Traveling in the Car

Remember, this may be your puppy's first time in a car. It might be very strange and a little uncomfortable to them. It is a confined space, and the movement or the sound of the engine could cause them discomfort. The following list is a set of steps you can take to help your puppy ease into the car and enjoy the ride back to their new home, as much as possible. Maybe one day, they will start to enjoy the sensation of car journeys.

Step 1: Introduce your puppy slowly to the car. While the car is stationary, let them sit, have a sniff and a little roam around the vehicle. Take them around the interior and exterior. Give them time to adjust to this new setting.

Step 2: You're ready to start moving. Place the puppy in the crate, if you have brought one, or make sure they are securely seated (either with a seatbelt harness or in the arms of a travel companion). Do not travel alone with a free-roaming puppy; they will be a distraction for you and could cause a serious accident.

Start driving slowly. Stopping every now and then, let the puppy get used to the motion. Always praise them for their good behavior. Once they have become accustomed to the movement of the car, start driving consistently. Talking to your puppy as you drive will help to soothe them. Reassure them that everything is alright and that they are doing great. Puppies and dogs pick up on your emotions.

Step 3: Drive gently and try not to make any sudden movements or drive erratically. Turn corners slowly and gradually slow down at stops. Speeding or unstable driving can upset your puppy's stomach and make them nervous.

Things to remember:

- If you are on a long drive journey, take a regular bathroom and fresh air breaks.
- If the weather is hot, keep the AC running or slightly lower a window. You can also purchase shades to guard the car interior from direct sunlight.
- Do not let your puppy stick their head out the window. It looks like fun, but they may risk jumping out or getting hit by a passing object.
- Travel with water if you're traveling for more than an hour or so. Stop when necessary to offer water to your puppy.

Introducing Your Puppy to Their New Home

With what was hopefully a safe journey back home, it is now time to give your puppy the best introduction to their new surroundings that you can. Your puppy will be experiencing an overwhelming mix of elation and nervousness; this transition will be one of the most stressful periods of their life. A whole new playground, new people, new smells, a new yard, new rules, and maybe even a new climate - it's a great deal for them to take in. It's crucial that you plan this part of their introduction. While you may view your home as a place of comfort and familiarity, it is very much the opposite for your puppy. Make their first time in your home memorable, in a positive way! Show them that this home will be theirs.

Making introductions: Your house is strange to your new puppy, and the other residents (either people or other pets) in your home may also cause your puppy some anxiety (don't worry it's only initial nerves). Eventually, you are going to tour your puppy around the house. However, rather than having a new person to meet in every room along the way, create a designated greeting area that will ease your puppy's first day stress. Find somewhere safe (preferably) outside the house; a large, open but enclosed space - a yard area with a fence surrounding it, for instance. Try to avoid taking your puppy to a nearby park, as it will likely be busy with people and other dogs. A park will also have been "claimed" by other animals, which can be intimidating to a puppy. Your puppy should be unafraid to settle into their territory and make it theirs.

Keep the area clear of any other distractions; no toys, food, treats or bed. Your pup should be focused on meeting their new housemates. Do not invite too many people, only essential house mates. Keep your puppy on its leash when you take them out of the car and have the rest of the family/friends stay at a distance in the yard. Let your pup find them, and go there out of their own curiosity - you can guide them a little if they are reluctant - but do not have everyone crowding them at once. If you have young children, instruct them to wait for the puppy to move over to them, and not to grab or shout at it to get its attention. They must respect the puppy's space. One-by-one, so everyone can make a friendly introduction with the puppy, have each person take a few minutes to introduce themselves. Your puppy will gain confidence in taking steps to get to know everyone in their own time.

Into the house: It's now time to show your pup their new home. If you have adhered to all of the preparation, this will be a very straightforward process. Keeping your puppy on its lead, guide them through each room of the house. This will help to control their excitement, and stop them from running around all over the place and getting into mischief. Do this alone; it is important that your puppy does not get distracted by too many people crowding them. Show your puppy their toys, their sleeping area, the potty area and their crate. They will need to adjust and become very familiar with each of these spaces. Close off any areas your puppy will not be allowed to access, and get them used to rules from the get-go. Don't confuse your puppy by taking them into a room they are not allowed to enter in the future.

Allow your puppy to settle into each room - if they choose to stop and play with their new toys let them. Give them room and do not smother them or prohibit them from exploring. Gifting a toy to a puppy will be a great comfort in their new house. They might choose to play, sleep, explore the yard or the room. They should be allowed to do this - as long as they are respecting the place and the things inside it.

Your puppy may not calm down immediately and this is okay - take as much time with them as they establish themselves in their new home.

Other pets: If you have other pets in the family, it is better that they remain separated as your puppy wanders around the home. The safest and easiest way to get your pets acquainted is by introducing them somewhere outside of the house (it is more open and neutral for both pets). It will also prevent your current pet from becoming territorial. Take them all for a walk in the yard, side-by-side, and let them sniff and take a look at one another. Keep treats with you and reward both pets for good and civil behavior, making sure your affection is spread equally between pets - it is not uncommon for older pets to feel jealousy. Your older dog may snap, or try to nip or growl at the puppy, this is very natural defensive behavior.

Under no circumstances should they aggressively chase or hurt your puppy. In the instance of a little confrontation, comfort your older dog, but firmly correct their behavior. Reassure them that the new puppy is not a threat. In my house, we have a spray bottle that we use to "discipline" our dogs. If there's a tussle, we spritz the dogs and tell them to, "settle down." They know this command, and that it means they need to quiet down. After they do so, we lavish praise on them, and say, "good dogs."

Establishing a Routine

Make training and routine consistent from the get-go; it is the best way for your puppy to learn the ropes and relax into their new life. Your puppy has just undergone a very stressful and uprooting movement in their life, and having routines will be their anchor. Your puppy must learn boundaries, rules and the way of life in your home. Establishing an order to their life enables them to learn good habits quickly, and it will simplify your life too. The older puppies become, the more they begin to test your authority, and develop their own personality. You do not want to find yourself two months into this relationship with an arrogant, unruly and misbehaving pup. The following points will help guide you through the first few days with your pup:

- Set up a walking, feeding and sleeping routine. Know in advance when you want your puppy to sleep, and when they are to be walked and fed. Feeding your puppy encourages them to walk, then relieve themselves or play. Completing these tasks tires them out, requiring them to sleep. Stick to the same times for this routine each day.
- Make sure your puppy sleeps only in their sleeping area. This will make bedtime run more smoothly, as your pup will know where their bed is. We set up a crate, with a cozy bed, and the pups quickly learn to love their little "den." More on crates, later.
- Keep your pup on an age-appropriate feeding schedule. They will need a lot of food to support growing; initially you should be feeding them three-four times a day. However,

this can be reduced to twice a day after the first six months. If your pup has been fed on a separate brand of food than you are planning to feed them, gradually wean them off what they are used to. This will be less of a shock to their digestive system, as mentioned previously. Start with ¼ of the new formula. After a few days or a week, make the blend 50/50. Then ¾ new formula to ¼ of the old food. Finally, 100% the new formula. This process can take a couple of weeks, so factor that in when you purchase puppy food.

- Make sure you and your family are keeping your puppy in line from the get-go. It is easy to say "oh, he can do it just this once" but once will very quickly become the rest of your puppy's life. Whether it's chewing furniture, jumping on people, biting their leash, or running rampant over the house, always ensure bad behavior is corrected. Decide on the rules, as a family, and on the words you'll use to correct the puppy. If one person is saying "down" for a puppy to get off the furniture, and another is using "off" for the same command, the puppy will be confused, and you'll all be frustrated. (More on training in the next chapter!)
- Arrange home care. Your puppy and your

household must be in a routine. You will be the primary caregiver, and hopefully you will have taken time off work to spend with your new puppy. If there will be times you're absent, delegate responsibilities to others. Ideally family or friends who know the routine and the puppy, or a trainer/dog sitter that you trust.

CHAPTER 2
ESSENTIAL TRAINING

It is no secret that our wonderful adorable puppies are messy. The first twenty-four hours of your time together will be a stark reminder of this. At first, they will leave puddles on the floor, they will whine and cry at night and everything they can fit in their mouths is chewable.

While it may be frustrating and a shock to the system, it's important that you remember puppies are not born with a natural sense of appropriate behavior, of where it is acceptable to go to the bathroom. Very much like ourselves, these natural routines require training, consistent guidance and repetition. The first training that you embark on with your dog must cover these essential points (sleeping arrangements, walks, potty training). Covering these will help to keep your home undamaged, and help maintain you and your puppy's happiness.

Potty Training

It's common for people to have a panicked response when they hear these words. How do you even show your puppy the right way to go to the bathroom? It is estimated that house training can take roughly 4-6 months; factors such as size and previous living conditions will affect how quickly your puppy adapts.

On your part, it will require patience and dedication; this training will be simple if you take the time and trouble to establish a positive routine. Accidents are bound to happen and making mistakes is how we all learn. Results will be best achieved by controlling your dog's environment and supervising them closely. As with all your dog's training, the best outcomes will be achieved with patience and consistency.

Let's get them house-trained!

Puppy pads

Before we go into routine, it's important we look at any equipment necessary for guiding your puppy to better toilet habits. All you will need is:

- Puppy pads or newspapers

- Treats to reward them for relieving themselves in the right spot

While it is preferred that you train your puppy from the get-go to go to the bathroom outside, a routine I'd strongly recommend, it can be difficult to provide bathroom breaks due to your schedule or living situation. The convenience with puppy pads is that they are easy access to a suitable relieving spot. Your puppy's bladder won't be very strong at first, and if you live in a larger house, or if your puppy is desperate, they may not make it outside on time.

The pads are scented and encourage your puppy to relieve themselves in an appropriate space. A puppy will want to return to a familiar bathroom spot, where they can smell they've been before. Placing one or two around the house (if you have a larger house) will limit their temptation to pee wherever they like. Ideally, place them close to the front or back door, regularly returning to that spot will indicate they need to go outside, and they will begin to associate bathroom breaks with that spot. Pads are also very easy to clean; they are highly absorbent. Some even come with holder trays that make cleaning up the mess easier on the owner.

Remember, this part of training will only be used at the very beginning. Puppy pads are a temporary solution and should not be a system that you or your dog relies on. As your pup grows and matures into better habits, the need for buying them will be abolished.

Signs that your puppy has to potty

Your puppy will begin displaying physical signs and behaviors to indicate that they need to relieve themselves. Observe your puppy closely, and look for the following:

- Whining
- Whimpering
- Circling
- Sniffing at the floor or carpet
- Barking
- Scratching
- Wandering out of sight
- Over-excitement
- Zoomies, or running around in circles
- Running to the door

If you spot any of these signs, immediately take your pup outdoors.

Potty Spot - On their leash, take them around the yard. Let them explore the space and determine where their spot will be (you can also introduce a spot if you have a particular place in mind). Once there, wait in that spot until your pup does their business. If they do not relieve themselves, take them back indoors and repeat until they catch on.

This all comes back to consistency and repetition for your puppy. Initially, you will be leading them to this spot on their bathroom breaks. However, in time, they will associate the outdoors with the bathroom, and the odor from their spot will draw them back. Your positive reinforcement can be brought in by praising your pup after they relieve themselves, either verbally or with treats.

Top tip: Try using a word as a command or a cue for them to do their business, such as "pee," "potty" or "toilet." Eventually, as you begin to take them more places, they will associate that command with action no matter where they are. At our house, our dogs know the difference between, "go potty," (which means to pee), and "go poops." Why the difference? You'd be surprised how many times, when they go outside, they run out to pee and then run to go back inside. But, we know better! So, we say, "Spot, go poops." And, guess what? They turn around and go poop. They weren't done. Dogs are silly!

Routine

Puppies, like humans, have basic needs. Our needs become scheduled, based on times we learn that it is appropriate to satisfy those needs. Getting your dog into this routine shows them that there are times to eat, play and relieve themselves. Without that kind of routine, patterns can fall into disorder, increasing the chances of more accidents and stress for both owner and puppy. Quickly establish when your puppy should and should not relieve themselves by following a daily time plan:

Waking up: During sleep, your puppy's bladder will have filled up. By the time the alarm clock wakes you both up, your puppy is ready, and sometimes desperate for the loo. Introduce a bathroom break first thing in the morning; no ambling around making breakfast, reading a news feed or checking your phone. Walk your puppy from their crate or bed, and take them outside. If they are very small, carrying them outdoors will prevent them from taking a detour to pee elsewhere.

Use this time to set up a familiar pathway and take the same route through the house and leave through the same door to the same designated pee spot. Instill some familiarity in your puppy.

After feeding: Feeding will become routine too; combining this event with potty training will get your puppy into a clean regime. They will swiftly learn that these two things go hand in hand. Keep each meal to a designated time as this will help regulate your puppy's expectations of when to await food and going out to do their business (i.e. reducing restlessness and accidents).

Wait between 5 and 30 minutes after meals to take your puppy outside; the younger the puppy, the sooner they will have to relieve themselves. Older puppies will develop greater control over their bladder and bowels as they grow.

Puppies will eat up to four times a day as they rapidly grow, and they will also consume copious amounts of water. Taking them outdoors after drinking is paramount, so treat this as if it were another meal.

Post naps and playtime: Consider a nap to be a miniature version of the morning routine; your puppy has rested and their bladder has filled again. Whisk them back outdoors the moment they wake up. Play times are active, your puppy is burning energy and their digestive systems are kicked into action. Afterwards, they will have a strong desire for a pee break.

Top tip: A puppy's need to eliminate is persistent, so keep in mind that a very young puppy (8-10 weeks) will require frequent breaks. They are too young to hold it in. In the first few weeks I recommend taking your pup out every 30 minutes to an hour. It relieves stress on them to suppress their bladder for long periods of time, and they promptly understand what you are trying to achieve. Garden/Yard/Terrace = Bathroom.

Rewarding progress: It is important to teach your dog the perks of good behavior; if you do not reward them for doing something right, they will have little incentive to repeat that behavior. They will never understand what is expected of them, training will crumble and it will take longer to instill good habits. Reward them with positive words or treats immediately after they have done their business. Remember to let them finish up completely first - do not show them treats or distract them too early as they might forget to finish and have an accident in the house.

Bedtime ritual: Puppies do not have the capacity to limit their food or drink intake. If it is in front of them, it is likely that they'll eat or drink it. To limit the chances of their needing a bathroom break during the night, remove your puppy's water bowl from sight. This will increase the chances that your puppy will sleep through the night. Should they alert you that they need an emergency toilet break during the night, do not fuss over them. Simply take them out and put them back to bed.

Regular feeding schedule and potty training: Giving your puppy regular feeding times is about more than keeping a routine; it also helps to regulate your puppy's bowel movements, which helps you to plan potty breaks more effectively. Feeding them at a consistent time each day makes it more likely that their bathroom breaks will follow a consistent pattern. As I stated before, feeding should occur at least four times a day:

- Breakfast - 7am
- Snack - 10am
- Lunch - 1pm
- Dinner - 5pm (this should occur no later as your pup will need plenty of time to digest their meal)

Puppy's bladder

Did you know puppies can hold their pee for one hour for every month of age? A three-month-old puppy would be able to refrain from peeing for three hours. This estimate will vary depending on breed and size (larger breeds require more water, so have a little less bladder capacity). As they age, their ability to hold in their pee will increase over time and reduce the risk of accidents occurring. This being said, puppies should never be required to hold it in, as there are risks of them developing...

- Urinary tract infections
- Bladder or kidney stones
- Bladder or kidney crystals

When your puppy is alone

It is not ideal to leave your puppy unsupervised for lengthy periods of time, especially in their first few weeks. However, absences are sometimes unavoidable. If there is a time period your puppy will be alone, always plan in advance. Make sure you take your puppy out before you leave the house and give them a chance to relieve themselves. Use the month and hour guide to calculate roughly how long your puppy should be able to control their bladder, but do rush back. Try not to give them too much space unless it is absolutely necessary.

Dealing with accidents

With any training process, setbacks are bound to occur. Your pup won't always get things right and neither will you. Mistakes are not always preventable. There are various factors that can upset a puppy's progress - a change in their environment, a disruption in their routine, stress, and especially fragmented training. After your puppy has a mistake, it is important that you handle it calmly and try to assess the cause of the setback; this will inform the best corrective measures.

- Is there anything you noticed that stressed your puppy?
- Did something occur that triggered them to have this reaction?
- Did you miss a "potty" break?
- Was their feeding schedule changed?
- Did they get into something that is upsetting their stomach? Has their diet changed?

How to respond in the moment:

- Do not shout aggressively, but make a noise to get their attention. A little "oh no" or a clap to make them stop. Never physically hit them to make them stop.
- Do not punish them verbally or physically. This will encourage your puppy to fear you, which is a poor dynamic from your relationship. Fear is not respect.
- Take your puppy outdoors as soon as they've stopped, so that they can finish.
- Clean up the accident with a specialized pet-odor cleaner to avoid a recurring temptation. Something with a strong scent can attract your pup back to that particular spot.

A pup may be prone to having accidents in car journeys, too. Always give your puppy adequate time on a walk to relieve themselves. Provide them with soothing distractions in the car; either a favorite toy, physical contact with a human being or saying positive and encouraging things to them.

Have patience during your puppy's potty training. It takes a lot of time and repetition for them to learn and practice good habits. Keep life as structured for them as possible and make the rhythm the easiest choice to follow. Keep an eye out for them slipping up or straying away from the schedule you've set. If they do, take them back to square-one and start again. It is trial and error, and soon enough both of you will fall into a successful pattern.

Sleeping Arrangements

Your puppy will be playing a lot, bounding energetically through your home and yard. Sleep will soon follow this lively activity. In the previous chapter, we discussed the necessity of breaking your dog immediately into a routine, and part of this routine will be settling your dog into a sleeping pattern. This stage in your puppy's daily life is essential, but difficult to establish. New puppies won't always take kindly to instruction and will require patience from you as they learn the regimen.

Choosing a sleeping spot

Take time and consideration when choosing your puppy's sleeping area. It will be a place that provides them with optimum comfort and security. There are a few factors that you will need to take into consideration when selecting this area:

- Once you have selected your puppy's sleeping spot, do not change it. Constantly moving your puppy from one place to another will bewilder them. As you are establishing with potty training, there is a designated place for your puppy to sleep. They will recognize this space as a place where they can have time alone, relax and be at peace. Moving their bed will leave them untethered and tense.
- It should be a comfortable spot; somewhere warm and without any drafts and safe from distraction. Your pup will never want to sleep in their area if people are pestering them to play. Over time, you can introduce your puppy's sleeping space in a more social area, when they are better trained. But initially you must make sleeping an easy undertaking for them.
- The temptation for your pup to leave their bed will be persistent. If you are not using a crate, setting up a few puppy gates around their sleeping area prohibits your pup from

wandering around at night. You can use a stair gate to keep them inside a specific room, or set up the penning fences. This way your pup can still see you and the places around them, as you help them adjust to increasing distance.

Dog crate or dog bed

Neither option is better or worse than the other, truthfully. Each comes with their own advantages and disadvantages. Remember, even after you have made the choice, your puppy's response might persuade you to change your mind.

Dog bed: A dog bed is essentially one giant cushion that will provide your puppy with a soft place to relax after jam packed days of fun and exercise. The comfort of a dog bed encourages good sleep. Having a soft cushion to rest on makes sleeping practically irresistible. As your dog ages, an accommodating bed like this will be essential for them. A fleecy dog bed will keep your puppy warm; this is highly important through cold winter nights (if your home is prone to drafts). The cushiony fabric will absorb your puppy's scent, so this will become their personal space - their territory and a place to chill out and snooze that is entirely theirs. The downfall of a dog bed is the openness. Yes, it is very easy for your puppy to enter their bed, but it is just as easy for them to exit it. A dog bed offers little restriction, which is enticing to a curious-natured puppy.

Dog crate: The aesthetic of the puppy crate offers up much debate about whether or not it is appropriate and comforting for your new puppy. From the bars and cage aesthetic you'd be right in thinking it resembles an uncomfortable puppy prison, but actually a crate can easily become a comforting sleeping space and a great mechanism for training your puppy.

A crate can easily fit a dog bed inside, giving your pup all the comfort it needs when trying to sleep. You can place a puppy crate in a more sociable area of the house, in your bedroom or in the kitchen. This way they will be able to see you, and be settled in your presence while still being restricted. Once your puppy has been bed trained with a crate, you can relocate it anywhere in the house - they will always see the crate as their space. Your puppy is more likely to settle into a sleeping routine because of the crate's restrictions. They cannot wander off, find things to chew or play with, use every square inch of the house as a toilet, or get themselves into any danger. Neither you nor them will be awake all night.

That being said, a crate can cause emotional distress to a puppy if it is poorly assembled. Make sure it is as homey and cozy for them as possible. Line your puppy's bed with something that is warm and soft, (either a blanket you've purchased or something the breeder/shelter has given you). Give you pup as much security as possible, whichever bed you choose.

The First Night

Your puppy has very recently been plucked away from everything familiar to them. This first day with you and your family, while being very enjoyable, is also a scary time for them. The nighttime comforts that they are used to have been stripped away; mother, siblings and a familiar environment. They will be feeling very lonely as nighttime approaches. Do not expect your pup to handle this very well on their own; it will be your responsibility to make them as comfortable as possible in this new arrangement.

Imagine bringing a newborn baby home for the first time. You would expect them to be restless, crying and awake through the night. A parent's job is to have patience and assist them in settling down. Puppies are no different in this respect. If your puppy begins to whine or cry during the night, there are a few options you can consider for helping them settle down:

- Comfort them in their bed or crate. Ignoring your puppy will not do. Dogs, like humans, are very social animals. Absences and time alone will make them feel uncomfortable. Companionship and empathy are at the forefront of their relationship with us. Eventually, your pup will have to get used to bed times (which will follow a consistent routine). On the first night, if you hear them crying, take the time to comfort them in the bed and assess the environment for things that may be disturbing them. Do not fuss over your pup, and don't rile them up. And certainly do not punish them; crying, although it can be frustrating, is your puppy's way of communicating their anxiety. The more action you take to settle their apprehension, the more likely they are to overcome it. Check in that they are safe and give them some kind encouragement to settle them down (praise or stroking them). Then, send them to bed again. Eventually, your pup will understand that they are safe in their new home.

- Separation can be introduced gradually. If you would like to wean your pup off company at night, you can try placing their crate or bed in your bedroom for the first night. Then slowly move it further from your bedroom to their sleeping spot. This method should be used as a last-resort, by the way. Ideally your puppy should sleep in their designated area from day-one, but they may find the separation difficult. This approach can help you make the change a little easier for them. If you are going to take this course of action, I highly advise using a crate. A bed with no restriction will allow your puppy to crawl into your bed and you will be up in circles all night trying to move them out. This co-sleeping arrangement may become permanent if you are happy to have your dog's bed in your bedroom. For others, it may not work at all as it is a personal preference you will have to navigate.

- If your puppy is not sleeping in the bedroom, have them somewhere close by so you can hear them stirring at night. It is very likely that, as your puppy becomes accustomed to potty training, they will have accidents. Hearing their activity at night will allow you to act quickly and carry them outside to the bathroom.

Additional tips:

- Make sure that the bed and area you choose has nothing chewable in reach. Puppies will be anxious at night, and chewing is a cathartic distraction. Keep your home and your puppy safe from this temptation.

- Choose a comfy and accessible bed for your puppy. No high or firm steps or sides; nothing that will give them any discomfort while they sleep or when they are getting into bed. Their legs, bones and joints are still developing; make sleeping spaces as easy as possible for them at this age.
- The first bed you choose won't be the one your puppy has forever. They will grow out of their first bed, either through size or wear and tear. It is tempting to buy your pup a bed that they will eventually fill out; but something so big means more room for damage and accidents. Give your puppy a first bed that will allow them to feel safe and cozy.
- Place your puppy's sleeping spot in an area where they will not be disturbed by people, visitors or any commotion. You will not be able to set a routine if they are constantly being disturbed.
- Be sure to properly feed and walk your puppy before every bedtime. Both of these tasks will leave them with a satisfied appetite and a strong desire for a snooze. The better you manage these, the easier it will be sending your puppy to bed. It will reduce the chances

of them being unsettled and hyper throughout the night.
- Give your puppy as much comfort as possible in their new bed; a blanket or a favorite toy may help them settle. Your puppy should not be too rowdy at night. If you give them a toy in their sleeping spot, do not interact with them during sleeping hours by playing with them. It should be there for them to play with if they need a little consolation.

Going Out for Walks

By the time you bring your new puppy home, they will be at the age where they are old enough to be taken on walks (roughly between 8-12 weeks of age). There's no doubt that the both of you will be keen to adventure with one another. Walking is a perfect cardiovascular activity; it strengthens your puppy's bones, muscles and heart. It is an essential factor in their daily routine. Every dog, no matter how little or large, must be walked daily. Remember, the location of where you walk, and for how long, will be determined by their age and how far along they are in their vaccinations.

Normally it is not recommended that puppies be walked outside until they are fully vaccinated, as it helps protect them and other dogs against diseases.

Prior to them having their full vaccinations, you can still take them around your yard. My recommendation for walking time would be five minutes per month of age, at least two or three times a day. If you have a four-month-old puppy, this will amount to twenty minutes. Make sure that you walk your dog in a suitable and closed area. Their first experiences should not be stressful to you or them.

You should not be over walking your puppy as this can drive them to exhaustion and dangerous weight loss. Keep in mind that young puppies are also highly susceptible to the weather, so they should not be out for prolonged periods of time in excessively hot or cold weather.

Collar and lead

Prior to walking your puppy you will have purchased a lead and collar. The collar will likely be a new experience for your puppy, so it may take them some time for them to get used to wearing it. If you have selected the appropriate size (or an adjustable collar), it should be sitting around their neck comfortably. Look back to Chapter 1 to find the best ways to judge this. Remember to keep adjusting their collar as they grow, and observe them for signs of irritation. Using a lightweight nylon collar will be more beneficial to your pup in leash training. It will not feel too weighty or painful on them, or something that may cause them to rebel against it. The collar should be barely noticeable to them.

You might wonder when is the appropriate age to begin your pup's leash training - the answer is immediately! Walk around your yard initially, with your puppy wearing their leash and collar. This is the best way for them to adapt to the sensation. Do this from day-one as it will establish good behavior when wearing a lead early on, and will make walking with them in adulthood less complicated and challenging. As you walk with them, there should be no tension on the lead - keep it slack at all times. Your puppy must learn to walk at your speed.

It will not be plain sailing; puppies are very mischievous when they want to be. Expect there to be some road bumps along the way (jumping around, tugging, biting, stopping to roll around etc.). Have patience with your excited puppy. You are dealing with a "child," after all! These things take time to perfect. If they begin to pull on their leash, stop walking, and firmly tell your puppy to "drop it" (a command we'll talk more about in Chapter 3). Wait until your puppy is behaving again before you continue walking. In Chapter 3, we will also cover the "heel" command, which will help manage your puppy's pace, and stop them from lagging or rushing. Keep treats on you during walk times as you will need to positively reinforce good behavior.

Walking Issues to Address

Where to walk?

When introducing your pup to the big wide world it is important that you do not deter them by overstimulating their senses. Overwhelming them could leave them feeling anxious or stressed about retrying similar situations.

Start by introducing them to a few short trips after mealtimes. You can easily walk them around the block or take them to a park that is close by. They will be small when they are very young, so try your best not to over exercise them. Build them up slowly to bigger walks. Initially, if you know of any quieter nature walks, take your puppy there. It gives you both time to bond on your walk, and attempt basic leash training without distractions. Shape their experiences carefully, so that they get positive benefits from them.

Socializing with other dogs

Parks and woodland walks are teeming with dog owners and adventurous dogs. It is highly likely that, when you take your pup on an outdoor walk, you will run into other dogs. Try not to feel apprehensive about this; it is a great opportunity for your puppy to learn how to act appropriately around other dogs and people. Encounters can be pleasant, and allow your dog to adapt to new situations and environments. Getting your dog to socialize in the first few months of their life will have a great impact on their future temperament and personality. Ideally you want your puppy to become a friendly, approachable and well-adjusted dog that enjoys the company of other people and dogs.

Without social experiences we encourage our puppies to grow up fearing busy settings, and they can display anxious or violent behaviors towards other dogs or people. So, start socializing them as young as possible. Take them out as much as possible to help them settle into busy surrounded areas. Do not overwhelm them, so take them to an area with little activity at first and gradually increase to wider more populated areas when they grow more confident. Let them approach other people and other dogs on their own terms. Don't ever pull them or pass them over to another person.

Observe your puppy for physical signs that indicate how they are responding to the experience:

- Anxious puppies will attempt to appear smaller: no eye contact, curling their tail between their legs or lowering their stance.

- A confident and relaxed puppy will have a strong, straight stance with a happy wagging tail. They will be more inquisitive to investigate new people.

Rolling in mess

My childhood was spent growing up on a farm. The puppies I had in life were raised there. Everywhere there were temptations to roll in stink; dead animals, cow manure, fox manure, deer manure - every pungent odor you could imagine. While it is unpleasant for us to deal with, rolling in a mess is not as simple as bad behavior. There is a reason your dog has a tendency to drop and roll in it.

They are following their ancestral instinct, a behavior passed down through the years from wolves. Packs would use the smells as a means of communication. What was causing the smell? Was it worth investigating further? Sometimes if your dog has been cleaned with scented products, it messes with their authentic smell. Rolling in something strong is a means of reinstating a natural smell.

If your puppy chooses to stop'n'roll often on walks, keep them leashed at all times. If you can see them veering towards a mess, use this as an opportunity to practice the "leave it" command. Tell you puppy to leave the mess, and wait until they obey. Do not tug on their lead to steer them away, as it may cause an injury.

Eating off the ground

Eating is not just a puppy's means of filling up their stomachs, it is a way for them to explore the world. That being said, eating garbage, poop, or discarded food is dangerous to your dog's health. To steer your dog away from this bad habit, reinforce the "leave it" command and by distracting him with treats on a walk. At home or in the park, use the following technique to introduce the concept of "drop it" to your dog:

- Give your dog their favorite toy, let them hold it in their mouths and chew it a little.
- In your hand have a treat ready, and command your puppy to "drop it" (their toy).
- Once you have their attention, show them the treat and tell them the command again.
- Once they have dropped the toy, say the command one more time to fortify it in your pups mind, and then give them the treat.

Always have a treat ready on a walk, so that you can practice the "drop it" and "leave it" command. If the technique does not work the first few times, do not lose patience. A good habit will take time to develop.

Bring poo bags and other essentials

Not only is dog poop very messy and a pain to get off your feet if you walk in it, leaving it out in the open is poor dog walking etiquette and disrespectful to the park and the public. It is also illegal in some cities, and can result in a fine (or even being banned from certain walking routes). A puppy will have to go when they are out on a walk, and it is your responsibility to clean it up. Always take doggy poop bags with you, so that you can dispose of their mess hygienically. This will ensure that other walkers can enjoy a clean space, and that and your puppy do not get into trouble.

When out on a walk, always put a collar and identification tag on your dog. Keep the lead at the ready when letting your puppy have some roaming freedom, or if you are practicing return commands. You are sharing public spaces with other people who may not always be dog-friendly. To you, a puppy is cute. To others, it is a threat or an annoyance, and they may respond badly. Out of courtesy, when people are passing, always place your pup on a lead.

CHAPTER 3
BASIC COMMANDS

Training is essential to every puppy. It is fundamental for several reasons. By providing your pup with adequate training you can:

- **Build a positive relationship with your pup:** The training period is a great opportunity for you to learn more about one another. As an owner, you will learn the process of your puppy's learning, and your puppy will learn how to respect your desires and expectations of them.
- **Help them learn life skills:** Living in a world of humans comes with a great deal of pressure for your puppy. Giving your dog an enriching

experience in basic manners will steer them to success when living in our world. Through training, your overall goal is to comfortably introduce your dog to the human world, and setting boundaries and appropriate behavior. Training reassures them how to act, alleviating any stress or uncertainty they may have. It is safer for you, them and everyone else.

- **Circumvent behavioral issues:** Training sets up a language of communication with your pup, giving them certainty and support. Take the time and trouble to invest in your puppy. Demonstrating how to act appropriately in our world, you are more likely to avoid problems bred through insufficient understanding. Dogs are normally punished for naughty behavior; truthfully the onus is on us to help them learn better. If your pup doesn't know better it is because their training was incomplete. You are giving your puppy the tools to be good, so make sure the learning is consistent.

- **Expand their social life:** As stated in Chapter 2, socializing your puppy comes with many challenges and pressures. A well-trained and reliable dog will be able to tackle stressful situations in a calm and respectable manner.

When you know you can rely on your puppy's behavior, you can take them anywhere in the world because they have the fundamentals down. We expect our pups to be friendly to strangers, but if they are uncomfortable or unruly, this will be near impossible to achieve. Good training will teach your dog how to accept physical touch, sit and wait, and grow in self-confidence.

- **Provide bonding and companionship:** The journey of guiding your puppy to better behaviors, giving them the happiness that follows adhering to basic commands, will solidify your relationship. When you can see the fruits of your efforts, a puppy that makes good choices, you will be immensely proud of yourself and your pup.

Training now goes far beyond what we can get our dogs to do, but what it does for them. An owner who uses a punitive tactic to teach their puppy good behavior is destined to fail. Attempting to become the alpha in your puppy's eyes requires you to assert a dominant footing. This can be dangerous and mentally harmful to your pup if your methods are cruel.

Yes, the aim is to command your puppy, and to get them to listen to you. But the way I will encourage you to try is through positive reinforcement. A type of training that rewards your pup for their good behavior; training that motivates them to listen to you. Using force will make them fear you. Terror of putting a paw wrong is not remotely close to what we mean by being trained. The relationship you construct with your puppy should never be based on intimidation and dread, but to harbor trust and appreciation. The attitude that you use approaching training will be a determining factor in this. Remember, puppies that are taught using positive reinforcement are more likely to be:

- Patient
- Self-disciplined
- More predictable and reliable with their behavior

With the correct guidance, you can form a respectful relationship as teacher and student with your pup. I want both of you to enjoy and thrive in this part of the training. Let's get started!

Punishment versus discipline

Accidents will always happen, and mistakes will be made. Perhaps more than once. Your puppy is not born knowing what to do, and it will take time and patience to adjust their natural instincts and have them behaving appropriately. Before I take you through the basic commands, it is key that you establish a healthy approach to disciplining your pup. This helps you to curb naughty behavior like a pro, without damaging your puppy's confidence or your relationship.

Earlier in the chapter, I condemned the use of force to instill correct behaviors in a puppy. This, however, does not mean that you do not acknowledge when they act out of line. Without demonstrating to them that there is a behavioral issue, then they will not know to act differently next time. Discipline should be:

- **Consistent:** Telling your puppy off for chewing your slippers on Monday but not on Tuesday will result in confusing them. Without pushing for the correct behavior, they will revert to negative behavior.
- **Immediate:** Disciplining your pup after the fact will not do, they will not understand why you are angry or why they are in trouble. Observe your puppy and only reprimand them if you catch them in the act.
- **Firm:** Under no circumstances should you hurt your puppy physically, or scream abusive words at them. You will only result in scaring them. Reverting to that behavior makes you unfit to have a puppy in your life. When a dog

sees you screaming, or lunging to hurt them, they do not interpret this as punishment for naughty behavior. They see it as a threat. Establish your authority with a firm "no" to indicate their current behavior is inappropriate.

- **Time-outs:** It works for children and it works for puppies. Giving your pup some isolation in response to naughty behavior will teach them to forgo that action, because they associate it with time out. If you catch your pup nipping or chewing, firmly say "no" or "oopsie" and then take them to an area where they can be left alone. I would recommend putting your pup in their crate or a gated area in the home. A time out should not last longer than fifteen minutes.
- **Positive reinforcement:** Rewarding good behavior is fundamental; it encourages your dog to do the same thing as before as they hope to be rewarded. You can do this with verbal praise and affection or by feeding them a treat.

The concept of positive reinforcement has been met with controversy. There is a great misconception that owners who use this methodology never reprimand their puppies; that they never say "no" and there are no true skills or lessons learned. A rewards-based training will encourage your pup to ignore unwanted behaviors, because these actions do not provide them with affection.

Using encouragement like this in training builds a healthy relationship with your pup. You convert what would be problematic behavior without using fear as an instrument. You help your puppy adapt and learn, without damaging your connection with them. Rewarding your dog in this way can be achieved with the use of treats, which is something I will discuss later in the chapter.

Setting realistic goals

Dogs are not circus monkeys. This chapter will not prepare your dog for awards in agility trials or set them up for talent show fame. Perhaps you had some inflated ideas when you envisaged life with your puppy. While I encourage goal setting (as it forces you both to be consistent), having lofty ideas can really hinder your puppy's success if your expectations are too high. Giving your pup an impossible first task, because you saw Lassie doing it on TV, sets them up for failure and you will consistently be disappointed. The crux of training is not to have your pup show off. Your goals don't have to be non-existent, but simply realistic. What you are going to teach them now will give them fundamental good behavioral patterns, so that they can be trusted in the world.

The first commands your pup will learn are:

- Sit
- Stay
- Come
- Down
- Drop it
- Give it
- Heel

Have an idea in mind about short-term and long-term goals, starting small and building over time. Observe your puppy's behavior and make note of things that you want to correct. The more you get to know your dog, the more you will see things you'd like to change. Not all puppies will learn all of these commands right away, and they do not need to. All you have to do now is stick to the essentials.

When to start?

In short, start training your pup as soon as possible, ideally when they are under three months of age (12 weeks). This training should be light and easy for them to retain. You have already begun to enforce some basic training elements (potty training, mealtimes, house etiquette and sleeping arrangements). Your puppy is constantly growing; at three months old, their brains are developed enough for them to learn the basics. Their attention span will allow enough time for you to run through "sit" and "stay." Remember, your pup is always learning. From the day they are born, they learn from their environment and circumstances. Their personalities are developing, and with that comes tendencies to be naughty. Starting early sets them off on the right path from the get-go.

<u>Top tip:</u> It can be easy to get lost in training, either through ambition or frustration. The following is a list of what you can do to make sure the process is always an enjoyable and successful one:

- Have patience.
- Do not overwork or push your dog (use short and productive sessions throughout the day). Ideally it should be no more that fifteen minutes a day. You can increase time as your puppy gets older and more adept.
- Keep distractions to a minimum; always train in a secluded and quiet area.
- Keep it consistent and integrate training time into your daily routine.
- Reward success.

- As soon as your puppy has mastered one command, move them onto another.
- Keep it fun.
- Be consistent with your language. There is a language barrier between you and your pup. They do not comprehend word variations and synonyms the way that we do. Choose specific words at the beginning of their training that you will continue to use.

Commands

Sit: Teaching a puppy to sit is one of the most valuable commands that they will ever learn. It will most likely become their default behavior when you suspect that they're about to misbehave. When you or visitors arrive home, or if your pup is engaging in an activity you disapprove of, commanding them to stop and "sit" will calm their excited urges. The times it can be beneficial to use sit with a puppy are:

- Waiting to be served food
- Leaving the house for a walk
- If you suspect they are going to chase after something (a car, an animal, a cyclist, a person etc.)
- If they are over excited
- When they are about to jump up on someone

- When you are attaching them to their lead
- When you are playing fetch

The sit command will make life for you and your dog much easier.

- **Step 1:** To begin with, give your dog incentive to sit. Lure them over with a treat, make sure you pup is facing you and ready to start. Take a treat and place it relatively close to their nose. You can also use a favorite toy as a reward. Move it in front of them, until they spot it. Do not start the command until you have their attention. They cannot catch or have the treat just yet.
- **Step 2:** Hold the treat slightly above nose level, so that they are looking up (but not craning their neck). This will encourage them to naturally find that sitting position.
- **Step 3:** Once they are, focused this is where you give the command "sit." Wait until they sit before you give them the treat. Do not throw it at them, but instead lower your open hand with the treat inside and let them take it. If they do not act after you give the command, re-catch their attention and say it again until they do.

Stay: As with sit, stay is also a valuable command that will both protect your dog's safety, and handle their impulse control. In the future, you will want to take your puppy more places. Having them know how to stay will make this an achievable goal. A stay command will come in handy when:

- You travel with your puppy to busy areas
- Crossing the road
- Staying still in the car while you clip on their leash
- Leaving the house for a walk

- **Step 1:** Follow the steps for the sit command, until your puppy sits. When they do, however, do not give them the treat you are holding.
- **Step 2:** Once your dog is sitting politely, give the command "stay." After you have given the command, take a few steps back.
- **Step 3:** If your puppy stays, praise them and give them their reward. If the puppy moves to follow you or moves away, say "no" to make them stop (make them aware that action is wrong). Try the exercise again from the beginning until your pup stays put.

<u>Top tip:</u> The more skilled your puppy becomes at staying, the further away you can move each time. Keep

the distance short at first, and give them time to learn. If you are practicing outdoors and using a lead, make sure there is a long tether, so that they can move but not run away. This will ensure safety and give them an opportunity to have a successful "stay" response.

As you observe your dog's behavior, look for signs or triggers that cause them to bolt. What brought about that impulse? This will inform you when a "stay" command will be necessary.

Come: Following the stay command is the "come" command. It is one of the most important commands, as it can prevent your dog from straying away into danger. Your puppy should know to follow you to keep themselves safe. Teaching this command when your puppy at a young age is crucial. The older your dog becomes, the more independent they become and teaching a recall command will be very difficult to learn.

- **Step 1:** Follow the steps for the "sit" and "stay" command. You can ask a friend to assist to sit close to your pup, making sure they stay in the seated position. They should not be touching your puppy.
- **Step 2:** Once your pup is sitting and staying, walk a few paces away from them. Keep commanding them to stay until you come to a

stop. If they do not stay, keep restarting the command training.
- **Step 3:** Enthusiastically call your puppy's name, followed by the command "come." Welcome them with praise and a treat. Remember to keep your hand open as you feed them the treat.
- **Step 4:** Each time you repeat this command, increase the distance between you and your puppy.

<u>Top tip:</u> You can develop this command as your puppy grows. When you are out walking with your puppy, use this recall to have them return to you. Increase the challenge by having other distractions around them (other dogs or other people). It will encourage them to filter out unimportant or stressful environmental factors and hone in on you and on the command.

If your dog runs off when practicing this command, do not run after them. They will see your chasing them as some sort of game. Stand still and command with a firm "no." You can place them on a lead and guide them back to the spot you were training them in.

Lie down: Another effective command for settling impulse control, and teaching your dog to settle their excitement. A lot of owners will find this a difficult and needless command, but I highly advocate its value.

Having your dog remain in a sit position for a long period of time can be uncomfortable. They will become restless and less likely to continue behaving. Lying down allows your pup to flex, relax, and stay in that position for longer. Lie down can be useful when:

- You're out at the park and talking to a friend
- Taking them to somebody else's home or property
- Eating out at a café
- If your pup becomes an office dog at work or if you are working from home

"Lie down" opens up vast possibilities for you and your dog, and makes taking them places a little bit easier.

- **Step 1:** Follow the steps to the sit command, but do not present your puppy with a treat once they have sat down. Keep the treat in your hand, with a little part sticking out for them to focus on.
- **Step 2:** Place the treat on the floor, with your hand covering it. At first your dog will exhaustively try to get at it. Keep telling them "no" and have them return to the sitting position if they stand up.
- **Step 3:** Give the command "lie down" or "lay down." Give them time to respond, and keep

repeating the command until they do. Remember, do not push on their back or force them down.
- **Step 4:** To encourage them, you can reveal the treat, bringing it up to their nose and then back to the floor, in order to demonstrate the correct movement.
- **Step 5:** Once your dog has followed the command, reward them with their treat or toy.

Heel: This command will direct your dog to walk right beside you, instead of running away in front. The puppy must keep your pace; stop when you stop and go when you go. Teaching your puppy to respond to heel will benefit them in other aspects of their training. Heel can be used in leash training, and will prevent them from pulling on the leash or chewing it. Heel can also be a means of walking your puppy off leash, as you know that they will stay close by. Sometimes owners can be reluctant to take their dogs on a walk, especially if they are apprehensive of them misbehaving or running away. Heel with help eliminate this impulse from your pup, in no time.

<u>Top tip</u>: Make sure you are in a quiet, and peaceful environment. Having no distractions will make learning this command easier for your pup.

- **Step 1:** Run through the "sit" command. Once your puppy is seated, place their lead on them and reward them with a treat. Keep your dog seated afterwards, with the stay command. Keep extra treats in your pocket.
- **Step 2:** Once the lead is on, and you are ready, walk with your dog. Take it slow.
- **Step 3:** If your dog becomes unruly or starts pulling away, firmly say "heel." The aim is to have them follow you calmly, walking side-by-side. Do not control them by yanking the lead. Have a treat in your hand to keep them focused on you as they walk. Show them the treat and say "heel."
- **Step 4:** If your pup does not pay attention, and luring them in with the treat doesn't work, start again from the beginning.
- **Step 5:** Only reward your dog when they are following your every step and your pace.

<u>Top tip:</u> Try stopping every few paces and having your dog sit and stay. The older they get, and the more skilled they become, the more you can incorporate and infuse various commands.

Give it/drop it: Sometimes your pup can get over excited with their toys, and refuse to give them up. It can be hard to keep playing these games if you consistently spend your time chasing them around the yard. Less time doing these fun activities mean less positive bonding experiences.

Remember, never chase your dog to get items out of their mouths. This will only result in their confusion. Using the "give it" or "drop it" command eliminates that confusion.

- **Step 1:** Have some treats ready in your pocket, and your puppy's favorite toy in your hand.
- **Step 2:** Call your puppy over to you, and give them the toy. Praise them for taking it. Let your pup chew the toy, but do not let them leave the training area.
- **Step 3:** With a treat in your hand, say the command "give." Make sure, as with all the other training exercises, that your puppy sees the treat and focuses on it. As you say the command, open your free hand below their nose, indicating that you would like them to drop the toy into your hand.
- **Step 4:** When your dog releases the toy, praise and reward them.

<u>**Top tip:**</u> Your dog may drop the toy at your feet or nearby you. This is okay, at first, if they are responding to the command. However, try to reinforce that you

would like the toy to be placed in your hand. As they get older, dismiss this action (don't praise or reward) and try the command, until your puppy does it the correct way.

Post Training Essentials

Praise your pup

When we pass our school exams, we celebrate, and we are celebrated. Show your puppy the same sort of respect for their good behavior, and not only with treats. Play a game of fetch with them, or spend time with them as they play with their toys. Take a walk together or chase each other around the yard. How you respond to your puppy in post training will impact the bond in your relationship. Be proud of what you have both accomplished and enjoy it together. It will encourage willingness in your pup to follow your commands.

Praise goes beyond the classroom; make sure you are responsive to your puppy's behavior outside of training too. This encompasses the fundamentals of consistency in forging good behavioral patterns.

Treats

Using a treat as a reward for training is recommended, but do not be afraid to alter this by using verbal praise too. You want to encourage a healthy reward system with your pup, but you do not want them to become greedy or develop an unhealthy diet. In the next chapter we will look at the nutritional value of your puppy's food, so that you can make a more informed decision about which treats are healthier.

CHAPTER 4
NUTRITION AND HEALTH

In the excitement of bringing your puppy home, it can be easy to forget about researching the proper health care your pup needs. Improper nutrition and healthcare in a puppy can lead to:

- Increased risk of diseases
- Prevention of diseases hidden to the eye (worms, cancer, etc.)
- Poor hygiene
- Distemper, parvo or other deadly diseases
- Stunted growth
- Psychological and physical stress

In this chapter we will look at the essential nutritional and healthcare your puppy will require. We will explore the process of taking care of your puppy's health, from puppyhood to adulthood. I will also address some of the more common challenges and issues. The worst thing you can do for your puppy is be misinformed. Without knowing the signs of poor health you put your puppy at an unnecessary risk.

Of course a vet will be best equipped to care for your sick puppy, but it is your responsibility as an owner to be aware of the signs. Nutrition will also play an important part in your puppy's development. This is the period of their life where they will be quickly growing; their muscles, fur, bones, teeth, skin and internal organs all depend on healthy, balanced nutrition. Getting them started on a good diet will bolster this rapid growth period.

Dog Health Essentials

Vaccinations

As with humans, vaccinating your puppy is paramount. It's something you should have done within the first few weeks of your pup's life, typically within eight to ten weeks for the first round of vaccinations. In the days leading up to your puppy coming home, find a local veterinarian who you are happy to work with, and book your pup's first appointment, before you collect them. It is worth checking in with the breeder or shelter you are collecting your puppy from, to see if they have already been vaccinated, as the earliest vaccinations can start is at four weeks.

Your puppy will need a second round of vaccinations, roughly four weeks after the first. Booster vaccinations will also be necessary at 6 to 12 months of age. As your pup grows, it is vital that you keep in contact with your vet for regular health checks and care plans.

Keeping up with regular vaccinations gives your pup the defenses to grow into a happy, disease-free dog. Additionally, it will stop your pup from passing on deadly diseases to other animals; vaccinations are not only for your puppy's protection. A vaccination will keep your puppy safe from:

- **Canine distemper**: Commonly spread through your dog's bodily secretions (saliva). Distemper causes depression, sickness, diarrhea, and discharges from the mouth and eyes. While mild cases usually see dogs surviving distemper, a severe case can be fatal to your pup.
- **Parvovirus**: Spread through fecal matter from infected dogs, this is a virus that can persist in the environment for up to nine months. Typical symptoms of parvovirus include heart problems, vomiting and dehydration. As the

white blood cells in your pup will drop, it leaves them exposed to other diseases.

- **Kennel cough:** This respiratory infection is a puppy's version of bronchitis. As with humans, the symptoms for this disease is a rough, dry, violent cough - it may cause them to gag a lot or sound like they have something lodged in their throat. It spreads through viruses and bacteria. Although it can clear up in time, it is still important for your pup to be vaccinated.
- **Leptospirosis:** The root source of this disease comes from your puppy's urine, or through stagnant waters from canals where there are significant numbers of rats. Symptoms commonly include fever, tiredness, dehydration and thirst, sickness and jaundice. If left untreated, a severe case can result in kidney and liver failure; this will be fatal to your puppy.

A routine puppy vaccination takes the form of two injections; these will be spaced out between the ages of six to twelve weeks. As your pup will not be fully protected during this time, you will not be allowed to take them outdoors to socialize with other dogs. Walking and training will have to stay in the yard.

If you are bringing your pup into a home with other dogs, make sure all the family dogs are up to date with their vaccinations too.

Grooming Essentials

Although your puppy is young and not tearing through parks or muddy puddles (yet!), grooming will still be a part of their daily and weekly routine. All dogs (puppies and adults) will require some form of grooming. As with a veterinary check, regular grooming maintenance can improve your puppy's health. While giving them a glowing appearance is a benefit of grooming, it is not the primary thing to be gained. Regular grooming:

- Helps your puppy maintain a healthy skin and coat
- Encourages good blood circulation
- Limits their chances of developing stress, and higher blood pressure
- Allows you to check puppies over for any physical health conditions (i.e. parasites, abrasions, lumps and bumps)

This next section will take you through all the grooming essentials to keep your pup in tip-top shape. While you can pay a professional groomer to care and pamper your pup, it can be a fun process for you to get involved in too. It is more bonding time between you and your puppy. Grooming is not just about brushing your dog's fur. It encompasses all aspects of their appearance:

- Inspecting your puppy's teeth
- Checking that their ears, nose and eyes are clean
- Making sure their fur is not matted
- Looking at the condition of their paws and claws

The amount of grooming needed per puppy will vary; breed will be a deciding factor in this. Dogs with thicker and longer coats will require more grooming than that of a short-haired breed. A puppy with longer hair will acquire knots and dirt more quickly. Observe your puppy; what do you notice about their appearance? If you have a spaniel or a basset hound, dogs with considerably longer ears, then you may need to pay more attention to that particular area.

Long-haired puppy care:

- These puppies will need daily maintenance
- Use a pinhead brush or comb to untangle and tease out matted fur

- Pay close attention to the back of the legs, ears, backside and the tail. As this is where a lot of dirt and knots will gather
- To brush the coat, sweep the fur forwards and then backwards, as this will help you to get to the tangles in their undercoat
- Take your puppy to a groomer regularly to maintain healthy hair growth

Bathing

There's nothing nicer than a warm shower. You can give your pup some soapy TLC, and they can thank you by shaking their wet coat all over you. It's a time that allows you to assess your puppy for abnormalities, and keep their coat healthy and shiny. Most puppies will not have to be bathed too regularly; once every three months is required for good hygiene. The factors that will determine how often your pup will be bathed are:

- **Fur:** Is their coat long (catching more dirt) or short and less likely to get mucky?
- **Activity level:** All dogs will go outdoors for adventures, but some are more susceptible to finding dirt than others. Dogs with clean personalities and behaviors will need baths less likely.

- **Health conditions:** Some puppies will have skin conditions that require they bathe more often or less frequently (usually with specific cleaning products).

If your breed of puppy requires more frequent grooming, always use a gentle shampoo. Too much bathing strips your puppy's fur and skin of the essential oils necessary for healthy growth. Too much bath time also causes skin irritation, dehydration and dryness.

Nails and teeth

The good news is that nails, through natural circumstances, are already kept in pristine condition. Whenever you walk your puppy their nails undergo friction that keep them blunted and trimmed. If you feel that they are too sharp, you can file or clip them, using equipment recommended by a veterinarian or groomer. Be on the lookout for broken, bleeding or ingrown claws. This is when your pup will need medical attention.

Despite the fact your puppy outgrows their puppy teeth, they will still need regular oral care. It is better for you to introduce this practice early to get them better acquainted with it (as you will need to do it often). Start by introducing your finger to their mouth, quickly followed by the toothpaste. Buy a designated dog toothbrush, either online or at a local pet store, along with a dog toothpaste. Under no circumstances should you use human toothpaste. Like with training, praise your pup for remaining calm while you groom them.

Ears, eyes and nose:

Your puppy uses these parts of their body for essential functions, so it's up to you to ensure that they are as clean and healthy as possible. A quick inspection of each area regularly will tell you of their condition.

Ears: Smell their ears. If there is a pungent or bad smell coming from them, this indicates an infection. A leaking ear, or any strange fluid, can also be a symptom of sickness.

Eyes: Your puppy's beautiful eyes should look clear, and the area around them clean. If there is a buildup of gunk or mucus, gently remove it with water, and a wet cloth or cotton ball. Allowing mucus to build up can lead to eye infections.

Nose: Contrary to popular belief, a clean bill of health in a dog is not determined by a wet nose! To care for your puppy's snout, make sure it's free of any crusty build up or thick, watery discharges. If these conditions are present, take your pup to the vet, as they can indicate illness.

Spaying and Neutering:

There are various health benefits of having your pet spayed or neutered. It is a process that requires minimal hospitalization and risk, and will positively impact your pet for the rest of their life. In short, both procedures sterilize your puppy. A female will have her ovaries removed, and a male will have their testicles removed. This means they will no longer be capable of reproducing. The health advantages for your puppy are:

- Living longer lives
- Less susceptible to specific cancers and urinary infections
- Your dog is less likely to stray away from home looking for a mate
- Females will not go into heat
- Males have less (hormonal) bad behavior tendencies (It does not fix all behavioral problems, but it will alleviate some.)

Your puppy can be spayed from as young as eight weeks old. However, it is recommended that you wait until they are six to nine months old. While adult dogs can still be neutered and spayed, there is a higher risk of postoperative complications. As I stated earlier the operation is very risk free, but your puppy will still need some post-operative care to help them recover:

- Restrict your puppy's activity. Discourage running around, jumping and rough play.
- Keep their incision clean; many will have a covering over the mark, but it is important that you monitor it daily.
- Keep them energized with a good diet, regular feeding and watering.
- Keep watch over them as they relieve themselves, and look out for any signs of pain when urinating.
- Do not leave them alone for extended periods of time.
- If you notice any pain or discomfort, call your vet.

Spaying and neutering your pets is also a question of ethics. While some dogs are bred, and sold into happy lifelong homes, not all litters are as fortunate. Having your pet sterilized will help to control the pet homelessness crisis running rampant across the world. Healthy puppies and dogs, just like yours, are euthanized because of the lack of homes available to them. The onus for preventing this is on dog owners, such as yourself, which is why I highly recommend you consider this for your puppy.

Signs of Health Problems in a Puppy

When it comes to pet illness, the most responsible thing you can do as an owner is educate yourself. You must become a pioneer in puppy health. Knowing the facts of any puppy disease will make you more equipped for facing these problems, and understand how to act. Through nutrition and regular health care you can help your puppy live the healthiest and happiest life possible; but that doesn't mean your pup will always be free from infections and diseases.

Factors such as breed, size and age can make health problems more prevalent in some dogs than others. No puppy, even ones from the same litter, will have the same health experience as the other. It's important for you to be vigilant. In this next section I will detail common health problems in puppies, giving you all the clues and details for identifying when your puppy is in good health or not. Remember, although I am offering you pieces of practical advice to help your puppy, always seek advice from a vet when your pup becomes sick. Never leave anything to chance. If you are even a little concerned for your pup's well-being, always seek professional help. The information I will give you here is a simple helping-hand for your puppy.

The Signs

Dogs are not so dissimilar when it comes to humans and sickness. The biggest disadvantage with your puppy is that they cannot speak to you to describe their pain or suffering. As a pet parent, you must become fluent in reading their body language. A puppy's behavior will change if they are ill. Much like us, performing certain tasks will become taxing and their behavioral habits will switch. Below is a list of symptoms that will help you identify if your puppy is sick or not.

- **Lack of energy** - All puppies are sprite and full of energy. As you exercise them, you can wear them out. But in time, like an elastic band, they will snap right back into zoomie action. With age, they will become stiffer and less active. This is a natural side effect of growing old, and not an issue that should be facing a young dog. If you notice that your puppy is constantly lethargic, walking with their head ducked down, and their tail curled between their legs, it could be a sign of poor health. If you notice this sudden change in your pup, contact a vet for advice.
- **Yelping or whining:** As puppies bundle around house and home they are bound to

pull muscles or twist their bodies in awkward ways. This can leave them in a spell of pain that will usually pass within a day or two. However, sudden pain, with no identifiable reason, can be an indication that something is seriously wrong with your pup. It could be a muscle, an injured bone or deep internal pain; it might affect their ability to walk or eat. If your puppy does begin yelping, or crying in pain, gently hold them and apply little pieces of pressure around their body, do not squeeze too hard, just enough to discover where it is originating from. Afterwards, consult your vet.

- **Bad breath:** Your puppy's breath won't always smell of roses, but a dog should not have a pungent or very bad smelling breath either. Bad breath can be an indication of many health ailments, such as digestive or kidney problems, and gum disease. Allowing bad oral health can increase the chances of these problems developing or getting worse.

- **Weight loss or weight gain:** Abnormal weight loss or weight gain in dogs should not be taken lightly. If your dog is on a healthy diet plan, meeting their dietary requirements for their breed and size, then neither of these should be occurring. These can be indicators of underlying health issues, loss of nutrition from vomiting and diarrhea, too much or too little exercise, or an insufficient intake of the correct food. We will cover important nutrition later in this chapter.

- **Skin sores:** Signs of healthy skin for a dog are pink or back pigmentation. The best way to examine the condition of their skin is by spreading their fur with your fingers, and looking at the skin beneath. Do you notice any crusting? Any abrasions from excessive itching? Are there any discharges from cuts or broken skin? Any hot or inflamed areas? These could be a sign of allergies or skin infections. You should also examine the quality of your puppy's fur. Their coats should always be thick and shiny. Problems may present themselves in the form of bald patches, broken hairs, fleas or dandruff. A dog breed with a naturally thick coat will shed; hairs will fall off naturally - this is normal. As you groom your dog, be looking for changes in the quality of their hair too. Perhaps it has become dull, brittle or matted. A vet or groomer will offer you sound advice about products to use on sensitive or infected puppy skin.
- **Thirst and dehydration:** With excessive exercise, it is natural for puppies to take in

copious amounts of water. However, if they suddenly begin drinking excess water, without any justifiable reason, consult your vet immediately.

- **Digestive upset and changes in bowel movements:** You will learn quickly that puppies are passionate about their food. They will rarely turn their noses up at anything. As you feed your pup, observe their eating patterns and appetite. Losses in appetite will be an early indicator if there is something wrong with your pup. Ingesting grass (a natural digestive aid) and regurgitation is common for puppies and dogs. However, if they begin vomiting regularly or show a reluctance to touch their food, you should take notice.

Bowel movements for your puppy should be regular after eating (i.e. neither excessive nor constipation). As a competent puppy owner, you will have to get comfortable examining the color and texture of your puppy's stool. Indicators of poor health problems will be mucus, blood or runny bowels (diarrhea). At times, these issues can be very normal occurrences, however as they can be indicators of serious health problems always consult a vet if they do not clear away within a few days.

- **Ear odor or leaking ears:** These symptoms indicate irritation in the ear, as infections can be itchy and painful. Have a look inside your dog's ear. Can you smell anything? Can you see debris or discharge? This is almost always indicative of an infection that needs to be addressed before it reaches the middle or inner ear.

Common Puppy Diseases

Now that you have learned key symptoms to observe in your puppy's attitude, it is just as important to learn about some of the more common health problems in dogs. As I have stated before, this is not a conclusive diagnostic tool, but a means for you to better understand your puppy's health condition. A vet should always be contacted if your puppy is unwell; never try to administer your own care. Seek the help of a professional.

- **Worms and other parasites (ticks, fleas)** - If your dog has worms, there will be visible eggs and worms in their feces. Their stomach may swell, and they can also display signs of weakness or depression. Fleas are also easy to spot visibly. Your puppy will be scratching their body constantly. The affected area may

have bald patches or irritated skin and you might even be able to see fleas when you examine your dog's skin
- **Vomiting, diarrhea, constipation** - What goes in your puppy must always come out, but always be mindful of how your puppy passes their food (or if they do not). Consistent regurgitation (vomiting) is abnormal; assess your puppy's behavior prior to them becoming sickly. Take a look around their environment, as they might have eaten something that has upset their stomach. If the problem clears up of its own accord, there is normally nothing to be concerned about. Try to keep your dog hydrated as they will lose nutrients through vomiting and diarrhea.
- **Dog obesity** - Dogs will always gain weight through muscle mass and filling out as they grow, but obesity will impact mobility and activity too. Regular weighing at the vets will keep your puppy on track for a healthy weight for their breed. Obesity can be reduced by regular exercise daily and an appropriate diet.
- **Bladder infections** - Urinary infections in dogs are painful and potentially dangerous. They can be identified by blood in the urine, a difficulty when peeing (straining or crying when they do so), or your puppy constantly

licking that area. Getting veterinary care is the first step to clearing this disease. Normal care practices include antibiotics, dietary changes and, in severe cases, surgery.

- **Stings and insect bites** - Puppies will be curious about the world around them, and will make attempts to capture and eat insects. This can lead to them being stung in the process. If your pup has been stung, you will see swelling around the stung area, they may break out in hives, have spells of dizziness and disorientation or trouble breathing. Applying cool water and ice to the infected area can reduce irritation, but always have your dog checked over by the vet.
- **Kennel cough** - This is a respiratory infection that we've already mentioned, transmitted between dogs. The key symptoms you should be looking out for are tiredness, coughing, running nose and eyes, and an aversion to food. Your puppy's initial round of vaccinations will be a strong defense against them contracting this sickness. If they do, take them to the vet to get the correct medication. Your puppy will also require an incubation period to limit spreading their illness to other dogs.
- **Arthritis** - This disease will normally affect

your puppy in their older years (however it is not unheard of for symptoms to appear sooner). Arthritis will hamper their mobility, and your dog will find it more difficult to move around or stand up. Generally they will become slower. This, unfortunately, is a disease with no cure. That being said, you can always make life easier for your pup. To slow the arthritis developing, your puppy will need a good diet, nutrition and exercise.

- **Cancer** - It's a disease no owner ever wants to confront, but learning to spot cancer sooner gives your dog a better chance of surviving it. Half of pet related deaths are linked to cancer. The clearest signs are unusual body odors, lumps, drastic weight loss, weakness and a loss of appetite. Treating cancer can be an expensive procedure. Only surgery can remove tumors, or medication and chemotherapy can be used to shrink them and manage pain. If you think your puppy may be suffering from cancer, contact a vet promptly.

Nutrition Essentials

Nutrition is everything to a growing puppy. Correct measurements will support essential bodily functions. If dogs have intolerances to some foods, it will be difficult to provide them with all the essential nutrients. However, there are always supplements you can purchase to give your dog the best dietary care. Dogs need six nutrients to keep a healthy and balanced diet. In Chapter 5, we will look at ways of providing food that will give your puppy the accurate quantities they need, in order to remain healthy. The following is a list of the nutrients your puppy will need in order to thrive:

- **Water** - It is true as the saying goes; water is the source of all life. Without it, life does not exist. Water can make up to 80% of your puppy's body mass. It is essential for carrying nutrition throughout the body, blood cells, regulating body temperature, breaking down fat, protein and carbohydrates for digestion and flushing wasteful toxins from their bodies. The intake of water will depend on your dog's activity level, and the temperature of the environment they live in. The good news is you can source water straight from the tap!
- **Protein** - This is classified as a macronutrient, meaning it supplies energy to the body. Protein is also made up of amino acids, and will help build up your puppy's natural defenses. Protein provides structure to the body, healthy fur, and strength to skin and

nails. They're necessary for producing hormones, enzymes and antibodies, that keep the body functioning optimally. It is vital your puppy receives amino acids from their diet, as they cannot produce sufficient levels in their bodies. When carbohydrates and fat are at insufficient levels, protein can be used as a source of energy and calories. Your puppy's body is incapable of storing protein, therefore it must be provided consistently in their food.

- **Fat** - Do not be put off by the word. Yes, an excess of fat is bad for your puppy; however in the correct dosage, fat can provide your pup with a direct source of energy. Another macronutrient, fat is higher in calories, in comparison to carbs and protein. Fat also contains fatty acids, which are essential for the construction and maintenance of healthy cells.

- **Carbs** - This macronutrient is a combination of sugars, starches and fiber, and will be a primary source of fuel for your pup. Grains will be a fantastic source of slow releasing energy to get your pup through the day. Carbohydrates not only give your pup stamina, but they are filling and can help to reduce appetite. It is recommended that complex carbohydrates (peas, beans and vegetables) are cooked in order to help your puppy's digestive system process them easier. It is important to avoid buying foods that contain wasteful carbohydrates, as they will provide no nutritional value for your puppy.

- **Minerals** - Minerals are micronutrients that help your puppy's health by converting your puppy's food into energy. Minerals are also necessary for the proper elimination of waste and maintaining cellular growth processes. A puppy's body cannot manufacture minerals, so they must be consumed through food. These minerals will be essential for bolstering your puppy's life functions.
- **Vitamins** - Vitamins are essential for many of the chemical reactions in your dog's body. These micronutrients also help regulate levels of other nutrients in the body. They boost your puppy's immune system, keep their skin and coat healthy, and maintain proper functions in your puppy's nervous system. Vegetables and wholesome foods will be packed full of these essential nutrients.

How to get your puppy proper nutrition

As you decide on your puppy's diet, you will have to ensure that they are receiving the correct nutrients to support good health. In Chapter 5 we will discuss different methods for feeding your puppy, in detail, but the following list will offer you some quick tips to make sure your pup's nutritional needs are being met:

- Check out the list of ingredients on the food packaging. These are included in order of weight, and a good brand will have a clear identification of each ingredient (instead of a vague description). Generic descriptions (e.g. "animal meal," versus "chicken meal") are unhelpful, as you will want to determine, exactly, what your puppy is eating. If your puppy has specific food requirements or allergies, this will be an essential practice when purchasing food. Knowing what is in your puppy's food is the only way you will know that they are getting the nutrition they need.
- Fat should be provided from a named source (see above). You may come across broad descriptions like "animal" fat, but it is better for your puppy that you have full disclosure when it comes to what they are consuming. This allows you to see what type of fats they are ingesting, as some can be healthy and some are not. You would not want to eat

unidentified foods in your diet; it is not good for your puppy either.
- Make sure the food is enriched with the right vitamins and minerals needed for puppy development. Some foods that are lacking essential vitamins (or lacking the appropriate dosage) will be fortified. This guarantees that your pup is getting the vitamins they need.
- A general rule of thumb you should follow is to buy the best quality food you can afford. There is a big difference between budget foods and premium foods. The first variety contains many filler ingredients that add bulk but don't really provide a ton of nutritional wholesomeness. Buying premium, while it may be more expensive, can be healthier for your pup in the long run. It can also save you money on vet visits, by avoiding obesity, teeth, skin and allergy, and other chronic conditions.
- When in doubt, talk to your vet and ask for recommendations. They will help you outline correct quantities of meal sizes for your puppy's breed, and breakdowns of nutritional requirements for your puppy.
- Never give your puppy scraps of your food. Not all human food is good for dogs, and there are ingredients that we ingest that are poisonous to them. This will make for a sickly

puppy, and encourages poor feeding behaviors. If you are going to make homemade foods for your puppy, you need to prepare them separately from your own, to make certain that they are healthy for them.
- Overfeeding your puppy treats is an easy way for them to develop poor health or eating habits. Treats should be used in combination with verbal praise for positive reinforcement when training. Try to limit their intake of treats to training alone.

CHAPTER 5
STORE-BOUGHT OR HOMEMADE FOOD

Choosing puppy food can be an overwhelming decision. With so many options on the market and different avenues to take, it can be hard making the right choice. Having covered the basis of nutrition and how this will impact your puppy's health, it is pertinent that you select food with strong nutritional value. This will ensure that you have a healthy and happy puppy. Store-bought foods are scientifically designed to bolster your puppy's physical development. Commercial products are where most people will turn to when feeding their puppy. It is expensive, but a straightforward and simple choice. The manufacturers have done the tricky work of sourcing a balanced diet.

However, store-bought is not the only option available to you. We all enjoy the pleasure of a well-made, home-cooked meal. It is a personal touch, knowing someone has worked hard to make something tasty for you. You'll find that your puppy also enjoys this delight. Making DIY food for your puppy reaps many benefits. It can be more economical; you will know exactly what is put into your pup's diet, and there is a broader range of ingredients to select from. Most importantly, you will become more adept in canine nutrition. It is one of the best things you can brush up on for your puppy.

Despite which method you choose, the fact remains that puppies need puppy food. It cannot be put simpler than that. Their calorie intake, and nutritional requirements differ from a mature dog. Whatever you feed your puppy must support this development. It is likely that the diet you set them on initially will last for up to a year. As a general rule of thumb, puppies are still puppies at less than one year of age. The larger the breed of puppy, the longer it will take them to mature. This will affect when you begin to wean them off puppy food and transition into dog food. A veterinarian will be able to help you decide to make these dietary changes at a later date.

In this chapter we are going to assess the topic of nutrition further. We will look into the different pathways you as a pet owner can take (homemade, store-bought, specialized foods etc.). I will shed some light on the pros and cons for each of these choices, so you can make a more informed choice about what you should be feeding your puppy.

Homemade Puppy Food

Homemade cooking for your puppy includes cooking their meals from scratch. It takes a great deal of time and dedication, and it will be a big learning curve as you discover how to resource and prepare the right foods for your pup.

As you embark on this feeding pathway I would highly recommend consulting a canine nutritionist. Even if you source the meals in your own time, their advice and guidance will help assess that what you intend to feed your puppy will support their development. A nutritionist will also help tailor the feeding to your puppy's specific needs. Some recipes, even ones that come highly recommended, don't meet the requirements. A nutritionist will keep you and your puppy on the right track. Whatever your nutritionist recommends should be cardinal, so do not swap out any ingredients that they suggest. You could be replacing something crucial with an ingredient that is dangerous to your puppy.

Putting together a well-balanced diet

With such crucial health pressures dependent upon diet, it is not a detail pet owners can afford to overlook. Before you consider going down the DIY route to puppy food, it will be useful for you to familiarize yourself with some nutritional guidelines for your puppy, in advance. Before you weigh the constraints of time and money when choosing your puppy's food, it is vital that your puppy's nutritional needs are being met. You will not have the suppliers to rely upon to source the correct nourishment for you. Having a broader range of knowledge on puppy nutrition ensures that you can improve the quality of your puppy's life. It is your responsibility to know what your puppy needs.

- The FEDIAF (in Europe) and the FDA (U.S.) both compile a guide to nutritional requirements for pets every year. This is a guide that manufactures abide by when manufacturing pet food. They provide in-depth detail about what adequate nourishment foods should have prior to being sold to the public, and that animals are getting their essential nutrients. The guide is available online for you to read and is a good reference point for enlightening you on puppy dietary requirements. Both organizations provide breakdowns of nutritional units compared to the recommended values. They take into consideration factors such as age, breed and dog activity levels. They also provide information about foods that are toxic to your puppy. It's important to learn not only what your puppy needs but what they should stay away from too. The guide will be an asset to you as you make choices about your puppy's diet (whether you use store-bought or homemade).

Pros and cons

It can be easy to get caught up in ambitious decision-making when it comes to puppy food. You want to do what's best for your dog; and you want to be a dedicated pet parent, scrutinizing over every detail. While I have no doubt that you will go above and beyond for your puppy, a little bit of transparency will help ground your enthusiasm. With each dietary choice there will be a list of good and bad points that you will have to consider. Having all of the information in front of you will make the choice easier. A bit of enlightenment will help solidify what method you're more comfortable with, and what you believe is best for your puppy.

Pros of homemade food:

- You are in control of the ingredients and preparation. Homemade gives you a hands-on approach to making your dog food, meaning you can regulate the ingredients building up their diet. You will have control over meats, grains, supplements, and other ingredients. You can map their meals from scratch, and have greater control over cuts of meat, where products are sourced and how high the quality of each ingredient is.
- You can address a specific need that your dog has. If you have a dog with allergies, then homemade food is a great option for your puppy. Some fillers and additives in commercial foods can cause an allergic reaction and you won't always know that they are in there. With homemade food you can eliminate dangerous ingredients that will harm your dog. Using advice from a veterinarian or dog nutritionist you can customize your dog's diet, and source specific supplements for specialized dietary requirements.
- No fillers will be added to homemade dog meals. A filler ingredient is an additive that artificially boosts the nutritional levels in your

dog's food (it could be fat, protein, carbohydrates etc.). In reality most do not have any true nutritional value. These will pass through your puppy's system without giving them any nourishment, as nothing is absorbed into the body. Because you are in control of what goes into homemade food, you can optimize nutritionally valuable ingredients and eliminate non-essential ones.

- You can give your pup a truly diversified diet. Feeding your dog from the same brand, and same variety of food for the first year of their life is hindering. There is a high lack of variation which is both boring, and limiting in dietary value. With homemade food you can vary the ingredients each time, and you can give them more options and make healthier meals all-around.
- The food is fresh rather than preserved. Despite being scientifically sourced and researched, commercial dog foods are still prone to incorporating unnatural preservatives into your puppy's food. This is what will help the food last longer after purchasing. As you can imagine, not all of these will benefit your puppy's health and the inclusion of them can lead to conditions such

as heart disease, diabetes. Homemade food allows you to select fresh ingredients, therefore eliminating the need for these additives. Fresh foods are as good for your dog as they are for you.

Cons of homemade food:

- Can be expensive to make. Despite the nutritional perks to satisfy your puppy, the economic drawbacks for homemade puppy food are the biggest ones. Commercial food, while it may not always be nutritionally wealthy, can be very affordable. Homemade requires that you purchase all of the ingredients and supplements too (some of which be very pricey, especially when you are aiming for high-quality products). There is not always an option to negotiate price.
- Can be difficult to strike a nutritional balance. To get your dog the proper nutritional benefits in your puppy's meal you will have to do extensive and vigilant research to ensure their requirements are being adhered to. You need to know the nutritional value of each ingredient and the quantities needed to match your puppy's needs. It is very easy for your dog

to develop nutritional deficiencies if you don't find the correct balance. At first, it will be beneficial for you to have a canine nutritionist approve your chosen meals and recipes.

- You need to be aware of unsafe ingredients. There are particular human foods that cannot be consumed by dogs (chocolate, nuts, avocado, garlic, onions, grapes/raisins, chocolate etc.). Not all pet owners are aware that some foods, while delicious and healthy for us, are toxic for your puppy. To avoid feeding your dog something dangerous, educate yourself on toxic dog foods. Never guess or assume that it's all well and fine. If you are uncertain or apprehensive, you can ask a canine nutritionist to oversee the construction of your puppy's meals.

- You could be feeding your dog too many/too little calories. Commercially prepared dog foods will provide a guide for owners to follow when measuring quantities for their dog. They will know the approximate amount their puppy needs each day. Homemade recipes do not always account for this information. This can result in you under or overfeeding your puppy. Always make sure the recipe you choose has provided this vital piece of

information, or use dietary guides to calculate it independently. Watch your dog's weight carefully, and adjust as needed.
- Preparation and cooking time will be required, and depending on the size of the breed of your pup, you may have to go through this process each day. With training, walking, and other lifestyle constraints outside of your puppy there is sometimes not enough time left in the day to prepare a homemade puppy meal. The time commitment is high, and if you do not bulk prepare food it will be a daily requirement. It is not as easy as scooping up and dropping food into their bowl; you need to shop, cook, ration, and organize storage. You may be very keen to be a DIY dog food chef, but do remember your lifestyle won't always allow it. Without the adequate time to dedicate, you could be damaging your puppy's eating routine and nutritional intake.

Types of Homemade Dog Diets

There are many varieties and meals of homemade dog food for you to choose from. There are sub categories and planned diets that you can set your dog up to follow. Each of the following will optimize certain varieties of food, to provide your pup with exciting meals. Remember that DIY food can be boundless; you do not have to stick to one plan for the rest of your puppy's life. Incorporate as many ideas as you want from each; try them out to see what your puppy enjoys and dislikes.

The BARF diet: This plan is more than just a comical acronym, BARF stands for Biologically Appropriate Raw Foods. BARF diets take your puppy back to the basics, as modern diets have evolved and taken domestic animals away from their natural resources. BARF recipes eliminate commercial additives, fillers, preservatives and necessary booster products and strip the food back to unprocessed natural products. This gives your puppy a diet rich in all of the good things (vitamins, fatty acids, and minerals etc.). BARF researchers have delved into the questionable side effects of commercial ingredients and the degenerative impact they can have on your puppy's health. They optimize natural food products that give your puppy the essentials to support development and bodily functions.

Raw food: Plans like the prey-model insist that dogs chomp down on a mostly carnivorous diet. It takes dogs back to a diet outside of the domesticated one they have been adapted to. This diet plan largely sees them consuming the meats, connective tissues, organs and edible bones found in whole prey. The anatomical design of the wolf (your puppy's predecessor) was built to feast on these components in the wild. The prey-model will see your puppy eating a meat-based diet (approximately 85% meat, 10% consumable bones, and 5% other organs). The prey model runs on a similar principle to the BARF plan (that your pet should be eating unprocessed natural foods) the BARF plan is tailored to an omnivorous diet, as your puppy will also be consuming vegetables, supplements and oils.

Vegetarian diets for dogs: More and more people are following the trend of the meat-free ethical diet, and creating healthy diets for their dogs, accordingly. As with any food choice, it is important that you supply your pup with all the essential nutrients; the good news is that vegetarianism is entirely possible for your dog to follow. Dogs can still get the essential nutrition they need from eggs and other plant-based sources. You must always be cautious that whatever is being removed from your puppy's diet (from meat) is replaced with an appropriate alternative. Remember, if you are choosing this plan for a dog, always consult a veterinarian or canine nutritionist as your puppy will likely need nutritional supplements.

Homemade Puppy Food and Treat Recipes:

The following recipes will be a helping hand for getting started in homemade dog food cooking. These recipes are simple to follow, and very good for your puppy!

Cannabidiol Treats (CBD Biscuits)

If you have a particularly anxious puppy, then these tasty treats will help. Studies have proven that CBD oils reduce the symptoms of depression and stress. It is a natural alternative to medication. CBD is very safe to use, but always consult a vet about healthy quantities before you feed it to your puppy.

Ingredients:

- 320g/12 oz gluten-free flour
- 65g/2.5 oz oats
- 130g/4.5 oz pumpkin purée
- 1 tbsp coconut sugar
- 1 apple, chopped
- 65g/2.5 oz carrots, shredded
- 65g/2.5 oz peanut butter
- 1 egg, whisked
- 45g/1.5 oz coconut oil
- 65g/2.5 oz cup water
- pinch of salt

- 100ml/3.5 oz CBD oil

Steps:

1. Heat your oven to 180 C or 350 F degrees. Cover your baking tray with coconut oil.
2. Chop up the apples, then peel and thinly shred the carrots.
3. In a large bowl, mix the gluten-free flour, coconut sugar and oats. In a separate bowl whisk the egg. Once you have done that, combine the coconut oil, water, apple and carrot shavings.
4. Combine both bowls of ingredients together, and mix thoroughly. Add the CBD oil.
5. Measure out a spoonful portion for each biscuit, shape them into a circular treat shape on the baking tray. Bake them in the oven for 35 minutes until they turn a golden-brown color.
6. The biscuits will need to be stored in an airtight container, once they have cooled down.

Veggies and Rice Bowl

This colorful bowl offers your puppy a refreshing portion of protein, carbohydrates, and most importantly it is jam packed with vegetables! It is primarily organic and natural with vegetables, and a very lean cut of meat. Your pup can dive into this colorful and highly nutritional meal at breakfast, lunch or dinner.

- 195g/7 oz brown rice
- 1 tablespoon olive oil
- 1300g/3 lbs ground turkey
- 390g/15 oz baby spinach, chopped
- 2 carrots, grated
- 1 zucchini, grated
- 65g/2.5 oz canned peas

Steps:

1. In a large cooking pot, boil three cups of water and cook the rice. The packaging will give you an indication of how long you should cook the rice for. Once it has cooked, strain the rice (if needed) and set it to the side.
2. In a large stock pot (or a Dutch oven), warm up the olive oil at a medium heat. Place in the oven the ground turkey and brown it. Separate and break up the turkey as it is cooking, it should take about 5 minutes.
3. Afterwards, mix in the spinach, zucchini,

shredded carrots, peas and the cooked rice. Heat the entire mixture through, and wait for the spinach to wilt before you remove it from the heat.
4. Leave the mixture to cool down completely before serving it to your pup.

Top Tip: You can cook one batch, and divide it up into portions. Be sure to mark down the dates on the freezer bag, before placing it in the freezer. Defrost it thoroughly, and reheat it for a minute in the microwave before serving it.

Meaty Roast Dinner

Another hearty meal for your puppy, with a variety of meats and vegetables. This is a great meal to batch-cook, and supplement your puppy's meals twice a day over two weeks. Your puppy will love this delicious and nutritious combination of ingredients. This meal will be high in protein, vitamins and antioxidants from the blueberries (these will boost your dog's natural defenses).

- 900g/2 lbs ground pork
- 900g/ lbs ground beef
- 1 chopped sweet potato
- 1 chopped apple
- 2 carrots

- 130g/4.5 oz kale
- 65g/2.5 oz blueberries
- 130g/4.5 oz brown rice
- 195ml/1 cup water

Steps:

1. Using a crock pot or Dutch oven, heat up some olive oil and cook the ground meats. The meats in the recipe can be swapped for others if your puppy has a preference or a dislike.
2. Next you will have to peel and cut the potatoes, kale, apple and carrots. Chop them into small pieces.
3. Once all the fruits and vegetables have been prepared, add them to the Dutch oven with the browning meat.
4. Increase the temperature of the Dutch oven to high for three hours. Give the mixture a stir and then cook it on low for another three hours.
5. When the mixture is half an hour away from being done, start cooking the brown rice (look to the packet for cooking instructions). Once the rice is ready, add it into the main mixture and stir it all together.
6. Leave to cool before serving.

Top tip: This is another meal you can safely freeze, or store in an airtight container to use later that day. Remember to heat it for approximately one minute after defrosting.

Store-Bought Foods

Commercial, store-bought puppy food is the more common choice dog owners will make; but as with any dietary choice, there are particular advantages and disadvantages you should be aware of. While store-bought is a quick and convenient method, pet owners and scientists have raised concerns over its contents and nutritional benefits.

Pros of store-bought food

- Nutritionally balanced to meet all of your dog's needs, store-bought foods have been designed by nutritionists and manufactures to meet all of your puppy's requirements. There are laws that manufacturers must abide by to make sure that their products are following the correct guidelines. They are formulated to have the correct balance of nutrients.
- You get serving sizes and portion recommendations, as well as a nutritional breakdown. Not only will you know the exact

nutritional quantities in your puppy's food, you will also be supplied with a portion recommendation specific to your puppy's age and breed size. This reduces the risk of you over or underfeeding your puppy.
- There are many high-quality brands to choose among that feature primarily natural ingredients. Not all puppy food brands are poor in quality, with fillers and "by-products." Many brands take pride in the quality of the ingredients they source; most corporations are owned and informed by dog nutritionists and are aiming to give their clientele the best diet they can offer.
- They are highly palatable. A good, high-quality brand will not only give your dog great nutrition, but they will also make sure the components of your puppy's meal are highly appetizing. It is not all kibble; puppy food brands have a variety of flavors and textures to appease your pup's hunger.
- There are specialized products on the market to address specific needs. Homemade dog food will have to be thoroughly researched for you to optimize a specific health benefit. This could include strengthening bones, thickening fur, or controlling weight. It is a time-consuming process and it is most likely

that your pup will need very specific supplements to support this development. There are puppy foods out there that are tailored to nature specific health qualities, which completes a big chunk of the leg-work for you. This is a more convenient choice if you have a busy lifestyle.

Cons of store-bought food

- Premium brands can be expensive. With quality comes a cost. For a first-rate food brand, you could end up paying between $3-5 or more per pound for a bag of food. Puppies are fast growers and require a hefty amount of food and energy to support this growth. If you have a large breed puppy eating four meals a day, the cost of this will eventually tally up.
- Foods may incorporate fillers and meat by-products that are not so beneficial. There is not always complete transparency between consumers and manufacturers about what goes into your puppy's diet, and how much of this is nutritionally valuable. Some ingredients can be non-essential "padding." These ingredients are further detrimental as many of them can spur allergic reactions in your puppy, especially if they are unidentified.

In this case, you must veer towards specialized premium brands that can be customized to forgo any allergenic ingredients and tend to have cleaner, overall nutritional components.

- Store-bought food has a very long shelf life in comparison to homemade food. When you open a large bag of puppy food, did it ever occur to you why you could leave it open for months on end without any spoilage? Manufactures will fortify their foods with preservatives to slow down the process of food deterioration. Artificial preservatives are unfortunately common in dog food, which can have negative effects on your puppy's health. Keep your eyes peeled for what preservatives have been used in your puppy's food, as they will not always be listed alongside the core ingredients. However, it is mandatory that they are stated somewhere on the packaging.
- High-pressure pasteurization is often used with inferior store-bought dog and puppy foods. This is a controversial method of processing your puppy's food, used to kill off damaging pathogens. This sterilizing process causes a significant chemical change, which can contribute to the deterioration of beneficial ingredients in your puppy's meal.

While the food is cleared of microbes, your puppy's grub will also be robbed of much of its nutritional value.

Meeting Your Pup's Nutritional Needs

Most pet owners eventually offer their dog a mix of homemade foods, treats and store-bought products. This is perfectly acceptable, and a great means of varying your dog's diet, as long as you are meeting the required dietary guidelines for your puppy. As you become more accustomed to your dog, you'll get a better idea of their taste and the types of flavors they enjoy. You can start out by experimenting with specific food brands you've researched, or by making a small batch of dog food at home.

When going for commercial dog food, switch between dry kibble and canned food. Eating only kibble can lead to digestive problems, and dogs that consume only canned food have been found out to experience dental issues more often than other pups. Additionally, "Obesity and dental problems are associated with highly processed manufactured pet foods, especially those high in cereals...So it would appear that commercial pet foods, all of which contain about 40% sugars and carbohydrates, are the main cause of dental disease in dogs."

A raw food and organic diet eliminates the clutter that is found in processed foods; but regular oral care and health check ups will help you to assess the impact of the food products you are feeding your pup. When in doubt, talk to your vet! This is especially important if you want to make dog food at home, but are not confident about the nutritional requirements, or the types of ingredients to add to a meal (or to avoid).

CHAPTER 6
BEHAVIORAL PROBLEMS AND DOG COMMUNICATION

To better understand one another, we must explore the depths of human psychology. It is our guide to identifying what people feel and why they feel it. Through it, we learn how to empathize and support one another to the best of our abilities. The connection you have with your puppy should be no different. There is a wealth of great information for you to utilize that will bring you closer to your puppy.

It can be common for behavioral patterns of dogs to be split into "good" and "bad," but this is a very one-tracked mindset to have. Nature is far more complex than that. The emotional spectrum that feeds your puppy's actions is greater than "happy" or "sad," "good" or "bad."

In this final chapter, I want to give you some insight into the psychology of your puppy's behavior. Communication will not be as clear between you and your dog as it is between you and another human being. However, knowing what is motivating your puppy's actions will give you a clear indication of what your puppy is trying to demonstrate to you. With this knowledge you will have the skill to judge if your puppy's behavior is ordinary or if you will need to show them some attention.

Each owner must try to understand their puppy's behavior from a canine perspective. We expect them to pick up on our emotions so that they know how to behave, but it is vital that you do the same. I will detail how your puppy displays certain emotions; what triggers these actions in your puppy, and how you as an owner should manage them. There is a language barrier between you, but that does not mean that your puppy is unwilling or unable to vocalize how they're feeling. This chapter will help you make that connection.

Common Behavioral Issues

Your puppy's behavior will be an indication that something is bothering or pleasing them. Even a puppy with no previous behavioral problems can unexpectedly turn. To us, the behavior is either "good" or "bad," but as dogs do not have a natural sense of correctness, or what's right and wrong, their behavior will be a means to an end. As an owner, it is important to know what your dog is trying to express. Below is a list of common behavioral issues.

Aggression and biting: Aggression is not always a full-blown violent attack; it can be actions as simple as growling, snarling, baring teeth, guarding food and toys or biting. A puppy with aggression issues can be difficult to train. As an owner you will find it difficult to:

- Socialize them with other dogs and people
- Play with them
- Discipline them
- Take them out for walks
- Have visitors around the house

Aggression is your dog's way of vocalizing frustration, pain, fear or anxiety; essentially it's a strong warning signal that something is wrong with them. It is not always an indication that your puppy is "bad." Your dog may be highly uncomfortable playing with other dogs, they may be overly protective of you or their property. Dogs are naturally territorial, so it is common for aggressive behavior to exhibit itself when they feel threatened.

Sometimes it may seem like playful puppy behavior, but leaving any aggressive tendencies unchecked can lead to more serious and dangerous issues later in life. Playful behavior is a very natural part of your puppy's development. It helps them to comprehend and interact with the world around them. As your puppy matures, these behaviors will dissipate, and they'll settle into a routine with good habits. Differentiating between aggressive and playful traits earlier in their life will help you to identify if your puppy has an aggression problem.

- A wagging tail, leaping, and bowing with their bottom in the air are general signs of positivity and happiness. These are strong indicators that your puppy is play-fighting. There should be no trace of defensiveness, fear or anger.
- Reciprocation from another playmate is a sign of roughhousing and game. You will also see your puppy's behavior contained within play time. They won't act-out when they're alone, or they will stop when others stop. If they do try to continue the game, making a loud noise (a clap) or a firm "no" will help to settle them down.

- Teething encourages puppies to chew everything in sight. A non-aggressive puppy will be happy to chew toys and will not violently tear them to pieces.
- Look for signs of fear or pain (pinned back ears, shaking, slinking close to the floor, a tucked tail). Aggression is a response to a trigger, and your puppy may have been startled by something in their environment.

What to do: The moment you notice a problem, it is important to modify your dog's behavior before it worsens beyond your control. You can help eliminate anger by:

- Socializing your dog at a very young age is critical. Take away their fear of meeting new people and new places as early as possible. Frequently normalize this event so that your puppy does not feel scared when it happens.
- If your puppy displays possessive behaviors when eating, stay clear of them as they eat. Giving them privacy to eat their food reduces their anxiety of someone trying to steal it.
- Reinforce the concept of good and bad behaviors with your dog. Scold them and tell them off if they act inappropriately. Help them

learn that aggressive behavior is not acceptable.
- If things don't improve, seek help from a pet behavioral specialist. I would consider this as a last resort to your puppy's behavior. As the owner and primary trainer, you should exhaust all options of what you can do at home together. If your pup's behavior escalates, having assistance will make all the difference in treating them. A specialist will be able to observe your puppy's behavior and make informed decisions on how to help.

Incessant barking

Barking is complex and has a variety of motivations. Dogs will bark for all manner of reasons from playfulness to defensive strategy. The more common triggers for your puppy's noisiness are:

- Play fighting and excitement
- Warning, calling attention to something or someone
- Boredom, seeking attention
- Anxiety, more commonly separation anxiety
- Acknowledging other dogs, talking like you and I do
- Over protectiveness

What to do: Always remember that barking is natural, and most dogs will enjoy doing it. However, there are some instances where your puppy must be taught to be quiet. Not only is the noise disruptive, but allowing your pup to continue this behavior means that you have not addressed the root cause of the problem. When your puppy's barking persists, try:

- Assessing what they physically need. Does your puppy need food or water? Are they requesting that you take them out for a walk? Your puppy may become barky if their needs are being insufficiently met.
- Bond with your puppy. Socialize with them to eradicate their anxiety and boredom. Walking them changes their environment. Dogs can begin to get vocal if they are cooped up too long indoors or outdoors.
- Use both positive and negative reinforcement. A non-violent command such as "quiet" or "shush" said in a firm voice will instruct your puppy to stop their barking. Do not rise to their noise, be persistent with the command.
- Take your puppy with you when you leave home to reduce separation anxiety. Can you take them with you when you visit your friends? Can they accompany you to the shops or to work? Do not leave an anxious puppy

alone for too long. Arrange daycare if they must stay at home.
- Familiarize them with their triggers. Keeping them in a play pen, move them to an area where their barking triggers are; for example, near other dogs, children, in the front yard, so they can see cars on the street, or your neighbors passing by. Supervise them as they become accustomed to these triggers.

As with all training, have patience. The worst thing you can do is snap or bark back at your puppy. Avoid yelling or screaming at them to stop their barking. You will only encourage them to bark louder or scare them; neither of which solves the problem. You want them to respect you, not fear you.

Chewing

When I was child, our family went through three couches in six months with one of our puppies. This can be a particularly aggravating and costly downside of owning a puppy. It is not necessarily an easy habit to break, but by no means an impossible one. Chewing has a deeper motivation than your puppy wanting to rile you up; for most puppies it is a means of soothing the pain caused by growing teeth. As with most behaviors, it is entirely natural. There are few dogs who do not enjoy the sensation of chewing a bone or a stick.

Chewing gives the teeth strength, reliance and shape. It is necessary and healthy for your puppy to chew on something. Your responsibility as an owner is to establish what is allowed to be chewed, and what is not.

Your puppy's chewing habits can have many stressors:

- **Curiosity** - Your puppy is learning about the world. Part of this will involve tasting and testing objects with their mouth to help them process what it is and what it does.
- **Separation anxiety** - If your dog is waiting until you leave to start feasting, this is a strong indication that they have separation anxiety. The chewing is an outlet of the stress building up inside them. Other displays of separation anxiety include crying, barking, restlessness and urination accidents.
- **Hunger** - Your puppy may not be getting enough nutrition from their diet, therefore they start striking out on their own to source nutrition and food.
- **Teething** - As infants do, puppies will eventually lose their puppy teeth. This will motivate them to explore the world with their teeth. Teething is very painful. The sensation of chewing is therapeutic as their adult teeth are coming through.

What to do: Some subtle and straightforward guidance can train your puppy to munch only designated chewing items. Consistently pointing them in the right direction of these items will help your puppy make better choices.

- Always have an array of toys for your pup to play with. If your puppy has ten different chew toys to chew on, why would they need your sofa? Providing them with a fun alternative is the first step in preventing this unwanted habit. You can purchase toys that are designed to alleviate their teething pain. Observe your puppy in their first few weeks; take note of which toys they prefer to play with and offer similar ones. Keep introducing new toys every so often, as your puppy will become bored quickly.
- Dog proof the house. Anything that is valuable and visually enticing to a chew-happy puppy should be removed from sight. At least until they have better control of their impulses. Shoes, blankets, cushions and the like should be stored in a puppy-free zone within your house.
- Discourage chewing habits if you catch your puppy in the act. You can use the "drop it" command to draw your puppy away from

what they are chewing. You can fill an old (clean) spray bottle with water, and spray your puppy when they chew. They will not enjoy the sensation, and will learn the connection between chewing and the spray bottle.
- Regular and consistent exercise will stop boredom building up, making your puppy less likely to entertain themselves by chewing on something of yours.

Inappropriate elimination

As we covered in Chapter 2, accidents in potty training are impossible to avoid with new puppies. Within the first twelve weeks of their life, your puppy will have little bladder control. However, the further you get into their potty training, the less frequently this should be happening. It can be disruptive to your household or forbidden in public places. If your puppy continues to relieve themselves inappropriately, there could also be an underlying issue. Initially, you should contact a veterinarian to rule out any health problems. If your puppy is in good health, their urination problems could be related to:

- Excited or submissive peeing. A house-broken puppy who inappropriately relieves themselves from time to time may have an

excited bladder. Your dog is responding to stimulus around them; something that overwhelms them with either fear or exhilaration. If you are reprimanding your puppy with an aggressive stance, or walking through the door after returning from work, and they inappropriately eliminate; it is likely that excitement is the trigger. Your dog may also be shy and timid. Submissive urination is their means of pacifying your anger.
- Incomplete house training. Your puppy is not the only one responsible for their behavior. If your training has been broken or inconsistent, then your puppy will be confused when it comes to suitable potty rules.
- Territorial marking. Your puppy uses the scent of their urination to claim what is theirs.

What to do: As I stated before, hitting your puppy is never the solution. Reinforce that controlling their bladder is good behavior:

- As you walk through the door, do not fuss over your puppy as this increases their excitement. Enter the room and avoid eye contact with them; try approaching them from the side rather than head on. Make the experience as controlled as possible. Your puppy will sense your emotions and try to imitate your behavior (similar to when they were getting overly excited). Keep this behavior up, until you have let your puppy outdoors to relieve themselves appropriately. This will reinforce the routine of bathroom time.

- Stroke your puppy under the chin, instead of on top of the head. The hand coming down on them is overbearing and can cause further anxiety.
- Consistent exercise and bathroom breaks will help regulate your puppy's bladder, making accidents less likely to happen. If you can, keep playtime outdoors, so that your puppy will be urinating in an appropriate place. Always praise your pup for peeing in the correct spot.
- Do not scold your dog; simply clean up the mess with a strong detergent (to put them off weeing in the same spot again).
- If the problem persists, seek further and more specialized training for your puppy. Their behavior may be deeply ingrained. Behavioral training will allow an outside perspective on your puppy's behavioral patterns, and will identify things that you may be missing.

Separation anxiety

Your puppy has spent most (if not all) of their life in the company of others. This could be their breeder, their mother and siblings, and then you. It is an inevitable reality that your puppy will eventually have to spend time alone. However, the transition can be dangerous and emotionally tiring, for you and your puppy. With separation anxiety, your puppy will become destructive and troublesome whenever you leave them alone. It is estimated that separation anxiety spurs on at least "20-40% of all dog behavior cases seen by experts in the U.S." (Schwartz, 2003. Para 1) There is a significant chance that the root cause of your puppy's behavior will link back to their anxiety over being left alone. Separation anxiety can be identified through:

- Your puppy will stress out whenever you leave them alone, pacing the room persistently, with an inability to settle down.
- Urinating and defecating after you leave the house. Similar to urinating with excitement, your puppy is overwhelmed by the stress of being alone and controlling their bladder becomes difficult.
- Consistent barking when left alone is another sign of this type of anxiety. It could feel like your puppy is screaming, shouting, and begging you not to leave them. They will go

from complete silence to an eruption of howling noise whenever you leave the room.
- Chewing and destruction is not uncommon either. Your dog will run into things, and sink their teeth into anything in sight when separated from their owner. The danger with this symptom is that they may self-injure themselves (break teeth, cut their paws, or choke on something small).
- Running away is another scary consequence of separation anxiety. Your dog might have a strong urge to follow you when you leave. Your puppy could make attempts to escape the house, or chew through the doors and walls (anything that is keeping them contained in the house).

There is no root cause of separation anxiety; each puppy has a unique personality background and previous living conditions. The following are a list of triggers that you may want to consider regarding your puppy's past:

- Living in a shelter, having been abandoned by someone dear to them.
- Changes in household and family members.
- Changes in routine. For example, when you rehome a puppy it causes multiple disruptions

in their life. When you return to work after those first few days their schedule changes again, and your puppy may be alone for multiple hours out of the day. This can trigger separation anxiety.

In the excitement of bringing your puppy home, these behaviors can sometimes go unnoticed. It is important that you incorporate prevention tactics into your daily training routine to help reduce the chances of your puppy developing separation anxiety. Teach them positive behaviors as early as possible. The following list can be used as both early prevention and as curative methods:

- Train your puppy to spend time alone early on. Leave them unattended in rooms for fifteen minutes at a time to familiarize them with the sensation. Do not leave them unattended for hours.
- Get them comfortable with their crate so that even when you are not home they will have their own comfy space to rest.
- Do not make a fuss over leaving or entering the house; show your pup that there is nothing to get worked up about.
- Exercise your puppy frequently. It is a valuable cure for a restless pup; exercise

reduces your puppy's stress and energy levels, the same as it does yours and mine.
- Medicinal treatment, as a secondary resort, can be utilized. If behavioral modification has no impact on your puppy, you can turn to medical treatment. Ask your vet for further details about suitable medicines and dosages for your puppy.

Other Common Behaviors

- **Jumping up on people** - While it may seem like your puppy is trying to greet you or show you affection, jumping up can be a display of dominance. Allowing this to persist enables them to believe that they are the alpha; training a puppy that won't listen to your commands will be very frustrating. To prevent this behavior, have your puppy practice the sit command when they see you, or when people visit the house. Do not pay your pup any attention until they are settled, and do not shout at them, touch them, or engage them in any way. Remember to always reward them for performing a command correctly.
- **Begging for food** - Anyone would be tempted and lusting after delicious food. An easy way

to keep your pup from stealing food from others is by keeping them as far away from the food as possible. As you and your family sit down to eat, place your puppy in their crate (or a penned area). Take them away from the temptation all together. Look around your home for easy eating targets (children with food, trash cans, leftover food in an accessible area). If you catch your puppy with something in its mouth that it should not have, then use the "leave it" or "drop it" command.

- **Chasing everything** - When you're first walking with your puppy in public, take them on the leash. Assess their reaction to the environment. Are they chasing after people? Cars? Cyclists? Other animals? The "heel" command and their leash training. Do not let them chase after the object they desire, as it encourages repetition of bad behaviors.
- **Digging** - This tendency can be disastrous for your garden or yard! The first step to troubleshooting this behavioral pattern is to identify why your dog is digging. The most common causes are boredom and curiosity. The best cure for this is to spend time with them; play with them and limit their alone time in the yard. Remember, you've adopted a puppy and not a mole! If your pup is digging

for the pure enjoyment of it, there is the option of setting aside designated digging areas in your garden or yard, so that they can happily scratch that itch, or dig it!

Canine Body Language

Dogs cannot express themselves to us in words. You'll never hear your puppy utter the sentence "I'm feeling good today, shall we go for a walk?" This does not mean that you cannot learn other ways to communicate with your puppy. Verbally, dogs are limited. However, over time, and through repetition of certain words, they will understand the driving emotion (and the sentiment) of what you're saying.

For example, within six months your puppy will associate the "sit" command with sitting down. The word "walkies" will lift their spirits because they know they are going for a walk. Talking to your dog frequently increases their level of comprehension. It is important to understand the non-verbal cues that your puppy is giving you. These expressions will offer insight into your dog's emotions. Even if they can't say it out loud, you will understand what they need.

Tail wagging, tail between the legs: A dog's tail is capable of communicating many things and is one of their most significant body cues. Observe the movement and position of your puppy's tail; these factors can depict their temper. A tucked tail is an indication that your puppy is afraid, nervous, sick or submissive. A vigilant dog that's alert to its environment will have a stiff and pointed tail. A wagging tail is usually a positive indication that your puppy is happy and confident with its environment. However, sometimes a dog wags its tail when it's nervous or afraid. Spend a lot of time with your puppy to learn how to read this particular signal.

Cowering and lowering of the body: When a dog is fearful, it will respond with its entire body. Their response will intensify the longer they are exposed to the thing that triggered them, so it is best to remove it or them from the situation. Fearful behaviors can quickly develop into aggressive behaviors, especially if your puppy feels threatened. Your puppy may freeze, effectively shutting down in response to a surrounding stimulus. They may shake or tremble, or slink low to the ground with their whole body. They will avoid eye contact and their ears will be pinned back. Always respond quickly to your puppy's subtle and obvious body clues.

Rear high up, front legs down (a sign of arousal or happiness): Your puppy could be crouching to play or in a roughhousing game with you or another puppy. It is a preparation stance for a happy leap, unlike a violent or fearful posture (an arched back or low, cowering stance).

Pacing: Pacing is when your puppy won't settle. Instead, they are consistently on the move, restlessly roaming around rooms. They pace for a variety of reasons: anxiety, stress and boredom are the more common reasons. Your dog might be seeking some attention, and need you to play with them. They also might be desperate to get outside to relieve themselves. Healthy amounts of exercise and mental stimulation in your dog's routine will limit negative emotions building up.

Spinning: As with barking, spinning can take many forms, each one indicating something different about your puppy's disposition. Not all of these are negative or bad behavior. A dog will perform small circles on their bed before nap time, and they may paw their bed too. Your puppy is indicating that this bed is their territory. They are creating the perfect snoozing nest to suit their shape.

Dogs often have bursts of excitement, when they are playing or out for a walk. This can also be displayed in the form of a spin. Before they relieve themselves, puppies may also have a brief sensation of anxiety, which sets them off spinning. This may develop into intensified feelings of anxiety. In that case, you should seek medical attention from a vet.

Lunging: Lunging can be indicative of two things; a dog may lunge for another dog in a play-fighting scenario. This is a healthy interaction and a sign of curiosity of communication (as long as it remains playful). Lunging can also be a sign of aggression. They may lunge at other dogs or people defensively, out of stress or fear (and sometimes over enthusiastic curiosity). This can be scary for somebody who is not comfortable with dogs. Your dog is trying to create distance between the thing that they consider to be a threat.

Understand that puppies express emotion and intention through body language and movement. These two mechanisms give you a better idea about your pup's wants and needs. Dog brain MRIs suggest that pups are capable of experiencing a whole range of emotions (something to keep in mind when interacting with your pup). Think about when you see someone displaying unstable behavior like shouting, crying, screaming. You respond internally with feelings of apprehension and anxiety. Dogs are tuned into the energy distributed through your emotions. They will pick on what you are feeling. If you act erratically, then your puppy will respond negatively.

Finally, understand the fact that dogs are social animals, and they model their behavior after that of another dog. If you have an older and properly trained dog, you'll find it much easier to get a new puppy accustomed to living with you as they can mimic and learn from your other dog's behavior.

AFTERWORD

A final word from me before you delve into life with your new puppy, which I am highly confident that you are prepared to face. My intention of demonstrating the gravity of adopting a puppy to you, was not to dissuade you from this enriching decision. I wanted to prepare you for what it will entail. Most new puppy owners are eager to find the perfect puppy, buy all the fun essentials and bring their new addition home. Then they fall short when it comes to follow through. A lack of preparation is devastating for both puppies and owners. My intention is for you to not become one of these owners. I want you to embrace the joy that comes with owning a new puppy; but also to realize that this happiness will only come if you are a responsible puppy owner by managing and observing your puppy's life.

Afterword

Now that you've completed Shape & Care Your Puppy's Life, you will have gained clarity and competence when it comes to building a life with your puppy. Every action and decision you make is crucial; from introducing your puppy to the family, to setting up their routine. You now know the important principal training and commands, and how to bolster your puppy's good behavior with positivity. And you certainly know that it does make a difference what you feed your puppy, and that you can be more involved and aware throughout this practice. These early decisions that you make, and habits that you bring into your life are the basis for having a well-behaved and stress-free puppy.

If this book has taught you anything, I hope, it is that life with your new puppy will never be the same, and I mean this in the best way possible. My aim was to enlighten you to the expressive nature of your puppy's personality, and allow you to fully understand the motivations and emotions behind your puppy's actions. I cannot express the significance of not only identifying what your puppy is doing but why they do it. Comprehending both allows you as an owner to correct issues in an informed and compassionate manner.

I hope that the way you view your relationship with your puppy has been altered. You are not simply an

Afterword

owner, and they are not merely property. Yes, you do have a responsibility to command them, but this will not be borne from a domineering standpoint. You and your puppy will grow and adapt to a place of appreciation and respect for one another. The foundations of this relationship should be positive - this is what will give you and your pup the best chance of having a happy and stress free-life together.

Your puppy will not be the easiest housemate to live with for the first few months (and I'm sure they're thinking the same about you). What my book has provided is step-by-step guidance for you to take them through this transitional period. Keep following the advice in this book; always be patient with your pup's progression, and delicate with them in their shortcomings. Don't lose your cool or start screaming like a banshee at your mischievous pup; you now know better for dealing with their wrongdoings. It is going to be a complex and challenging time with your puppy. But what you have hopefully learned from my teachings will support you as you approach this new chapter in your life with gusto!

Best of luck with your new puppy! Thank you for welcoming a new life into your home.

REFERENCES

Kramer, M, H. (2019, October). Dog Breeder Career Profile: https://www.thebalancecareers.com/dog-breeder-125875#:~:text=Dog%20breeders%20are%20responsible%20for,companion%20animals%2C%20or%20breeding%20stock.

Kutsumi, A., Nagasawa., M, Ohta., Ohtani, N. (s012, January). *Importance of Puppy Training for Future Behavior of the Dog: https://www.researchgate.net/ publication/231224999_Importance_of_Puppy_Training_for _Future_Behavior_of_the_Dog*

Schwartz, S. (2003, June). *AVMA Collections Canine Anxiety Disorders:* https://www.avma.org/journals/collections/avma-collections-canine-anxiety-disorders

References

Winsome Speaking. (n.d.). *Dogs Do speak, But Only to Those Who Know How to Listen:* https://winsomespeaking.com/2019/02/19/dogs-do-speak-but-only-to-those-who-know-how-to-listen

www.ingramcontent.com/pod-product-compliance
Lightning Source LLC
Chambersburg PA
CBHW021438080526
44588CB00009B/580